QNI Quality of Nationality Index

1st Edition · 2011 – 2015

Quality of the world's nationalities in 2015

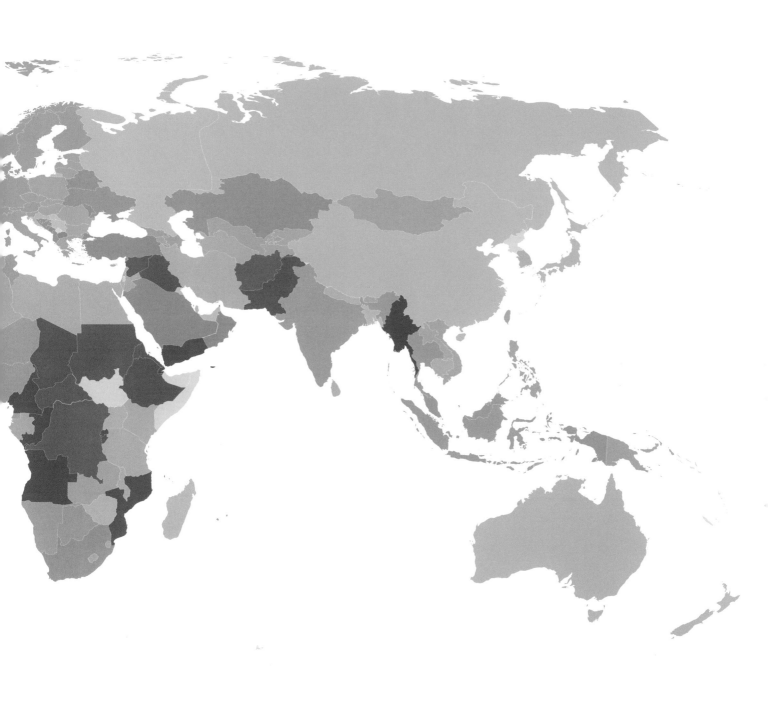

| Very high quality | High quality | Medium quality | Low quality | Insufficient data |

Henley & Partners · Dimitry Kochenov

QNI Quality of Nationality Index

1ˢᵗ Edition · 2011 – 2015

The Henley & Partners - Kochenov Quality of Nationality Index (QNI) is designed to rank the objective value of world nationalities, as legal statuses of attachment to states, approached from the point of view of empowering mobile individuals interested in taking control of their lives. The QNI looks beyond simple visa-free tourist or business travel and takes a number of other crucial factors into account: those that make one nationality better than another in terms of legal status in which to develop your talents and business.

Edited by Dimitry Kochenov with the assistance of Justin Lindeboom

IDEOS

New York · London · Zurich · Hong Kong

ISBN (Paperback):   978-0-9935866-0-6
ISBN (eBook):   978-0-9935866-1-3

"Remember your humanity and forget the rest"

Albert Einstein

Contents

Part 3

Expert Commentary

Annex

Glossary of Terms

INTRODUCTION

The Henley & Partners – Kochenov Quality of Nationality Index 2015

The Henley & Partners – Kochenov Quality of Nationality Index (QNI) is designed to rank the objective value of world nationalities, as legal statuses of attachment to states, approached from the point of view of empowering mobile individuals interested in taking control of their lives. The QNI looks beyond simple visa-free tourist or business travel and takes a number of other crucial factors into account: those that make one nationality better than another in terms of legal status in which to develop your talents and business.

The QNI ranks nationalities – the legal statuses of attachment to states – rather than states *per se*, taking into account the increase in world migration flows as well as the lack of a correlation between the nationality held by a growing number of active individuals and the countries where their businesses are established and their lives are lived. This is a fundamental difference to the absolute majority of other indexes and rankings, which take states – sovereign territorial entities – somewhat too seriously. In today's globalized world, the legal status of millions of nationals extends their opportunities and desires far beyond their countries of origin: the confines of the state are simply not the limit of one's ambitions and expectations.

Nationalities diverge strongly in their practical value – and this value is not always reflected in basic characteristics like economic strength or the level of development of the countries with which such nationalities are associated. Economically strong countries can have relatively unattractive nationalities (such as China and the Chinese nationality, for instance) and micro-states can offer nationalities of great value (such as Liechtenstein and the Liechtenstein nationality). It is not a secret that our nationalities have a direct impact on our lifestyles, freedom to think independently, do business, and live longer, healthier, and more rewarding lives. While the extremes are well-known – a child in Somalia or the Democratic Republic of Congo is 50 times more likely not to survive the first five years of life than a child in Japan or Finland; or Liberians and North Koreans are infinitely less likely to experience Paris, New York or Moscow than, say, Singaporeans and Argentineans – a single source that ranks the worth of nationalities is missing. This new index provides this single source.

The reality that the QNI describes is in many respects regrettable: in the absolute majority of circumstances our nationality plays an important role in establishing a highly irrational ceiling for our opportunities and aspirations, reflecting the core aspect of being a national of some place, which is a random act of birth boasting no correlation with any person's achievements, ideas, feelings and desires – "a birthright lottery" in the memorable phrase of Aylet Shachar. This is something that the designers of the index do not endorse, but observe as part of the day-to-day reality, which the index aims to document. The QNI, updated annually, is the source of a dynamic understanding of the quality of world nationalities measured based on a set of clear and transparent criteria.

The QNI in a nutshell

Everyone has a nationality (citizenship) of one or more states. States differ to a great degree – Russia is huge, Swaziland is small; Luxembourg is rich, Mongolia is less so. Just as the states differ, so too do the nationalities themselves. The key premise of the Henley & Partners – Kochenov Index is that it is possible to compare the relative worth of nationalities – as opposed to, simply, countries.

For a reliable comparison both internal and external factors are important. Internally, we look at how successful the country is in terms of human development, economic prosperity, and stability and peace. It is better to have a nationality of a country with long life expectancy, a good schooling system and a high level of prosperity – like Australia – than of a country which offers lower levels of security, schooling and health to its nationals – like Ukraine. It is better to have a nationality and as a consequence, enjoy the rights to work and reside, in a country with a large economy – like the US – than in a tiny country, however prosperous, like San Marino. It is better to have a nationality of a peaceful and stable country, like Denmark, than of a country with security risks, like Venezuela. These are the three internal factors that the QNI takes into account:

- Economic strength

- Human development

- Peace and stability

External factors are no less important, however: some nationalities give their passport holders the ability to travel around nearly all the world unobstructed by visa requirements, no questions asked – think of the German nationality, for instance – while others make tourist and business travel dependent on acquiring endless visas, or at times, *de facto* impossible – think of Turkmenistan.

More importantly, however, some nationalities come with a right to be welcomed by other countries and societies – a right to 'home' treatment. In this sense, possessing one nationality can amount to enjoying plentiful rights, including work and settlement, in a number of states, not just one. The Liechtenstein nationality, although conferred by a tiny country, gives its bearers full access to all the European Union (EU) Member States and all the countries of the European Economic Area: Liechtensteiners are equally at home in 31 countries, enjoying all the rights which the bearers of the local nationalities there enjoy. Compare this with Canadian nationality – which is associated with no such extra-territorial rights at all and the difference becomes clear.

Two external aspects of any nationality's worth are thus of importance:

· Travel freedom

· Settlement freedom with which each nationality is associated

To reflect the added value of both in the best possible way, the QNI looks at two criteria. The first is the sheer number of other jurisdictions where one can travel to or settle in while holding a particular nationality – Liechtenstein is then better than Canada and Germany is better than Turkmenistan, because diversity of the places you can visit or live in through your nationality matters. The second is what kind of countries exactly one can travel to or settle in with a particular nationality, taking human development and economic strength of every possible destination into account. In this sense, being able to travel to France visa-free is of higher added value than being able to visit Syria visa-free. The same with settlement: having the unconditional right to work and live in Germany which is associated with an Icelandic nationality, for instance, places Icelanders above Chinese nationals, since Chinese nationality does not allow settlement and work even in the totality of the territory of the issuing state itself.

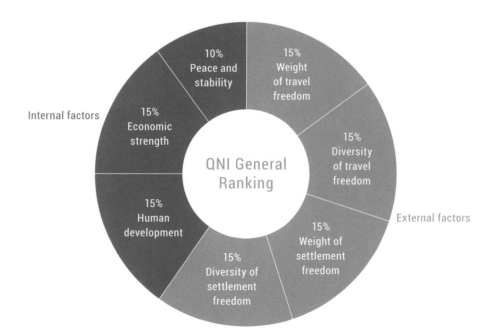

All these factors considered, the QNI is born: the Henley & Partners – Kochenov Index allows for objective and impartial comparative assessment of the worth of all the nationalities in the world taking both internal and, crucially, external factors into account. This produces a clear account of which nationalities are objectively better than others, working against two unhelpful mythologies. Firstly, it proves that one cannot possibly be correct in stating that any nationality and any passport is equally fine. This is not the case. Secondly, it proves that it is not true that the most prosperous and economically important countries will provide their nationals with the best nationality: while China is an economic giant, its nationality has a very modest objective value. Some passports are great, while others are quite simply terrible. Now we know which one is which.

The QNI divides the nationalities of the world into four tiers based on quality: Very High Quality, High Quality, Medium Quality, and Low Quality: giving a very clear picture of the standing of each nationality of the world at one glance.

Updating this index annually will make sure that an up-to-date picture of the quality of world nationalities is readily available at any moment in time, illuminating medium- to long-term trends in nationalities' development.

About the creators

The Henley & Partners – Kochenov Quality of Nationality Index is the result of a successful cooperation of Henley & Partners, the global leaders in residence and citizenship planning, and Professor Dimitry Kochenov, a legal academic who has been writing about citizenship and teaching nationality and immigration law and policy for more than a decade. The QNI blends Henley & Partners' own Visa Restrictions Index and Professor Kochenov's ideas to create a truly reliable and transparent measurement tool. Countless experts have been consulted to make this index possible. We would like to thank, in particular, Diego Acosta Arcarazo, Laure Delcour, Suelen Haidar, Borek Janeček, Justin Lindeboom (who did the majority of hands-on editing), Alan Murray Hayden, Greg Nizhnikaŭ, Gerard Prinsen, Aaron Ramos, Suryapratim Roy and Shu Yu.

Christian H. Kalin

Christian H. Kälin, TEP, IMCM, is the Chairman of Henley & Partners. After completing Zurich Business School and his training at a Swiss private bank, he lived and studied for many years in France, the US, New Zealand and Switzerland. A holder of cum laude Master's and PhD degrees in law from the University of Zurich, he is a frequent writer and speaker on residence and citizenship-by-investment and advises key clients as well as governments in those areas. He is the author of the Global Residence and Citizenship Handbook, editor of the Switzerland Business & Investment Handbook as well as numerous other publications.

Prof. Dr. Dimitry Kochenov

Professor Kochenov holds a Chair in EU Constitutional Law at the University of Groningen, is a Visiting Professor of the College of Europe (Natolin) and the Chairman of the Investment Migration Council. During the 2015–2016 academic year Dimitry is the Martin and Kathleen Crane Fellow in Law and Public Affairs at the Woodrow Wilson School at Princeton. He has published widely on different aspects of comparative and European citizenship law, and migration regulation, and consults governments and international organizations on EU Constitutional Law and citizenship issues.

Part 1

METHODOLOGY

1 Introduction to the methodology

The Henley & Partners – Kochenov Quality of Nationality Index provides a comprehensive ranking of the quality of nationalities worldwide. An unprecedented variety and depth of sources have been used to gauge the opportunities and limitations that our nationalities impose on us. For that purpose, the QNI measures both the internal value of nationality, which refers to the quality of life within a nationality's country of origin, and the external value of nationality, which identifies the diversity and quality of opportunities that nationalities allow us to pursue outside our countries of origin. Since virtually all the nationalities allow their holders to travel abroad and, moreover, a significant number of nationalities allow the holders to work and live in different countries abroad as well, the value of having a particular nationality can no longer be based on the qualities of the issuing country itself – indeed this is the core thought behind the QNI. All the sources used are objectively verifiable and build on the data collected by the leading international institutions with impeccable reputation.

The internal value of nationalities is calculated on the basis of three sub-elements: the economic strength of the country granting nationality in terms of its Gross Domestic Product (GDP), its level of basic human development expressed by the United Nations (UN) Development Programme Human Development Index (HDI) and its level of peace and stability according to the Global Peace Index (GPI) published by the Institute for Economics and Peace. Internal value relates to the practical value of a legal status for all nationals of a particular state or territory, including those who "stay at home" all of their lives. From frequently traveling businessmen to caring mothers and coffee-sipping hipsters, each of us is affected by the quality of the most fundamental aspects of our home countries. The more opportunities each state offers to its nationals through wealth, security, schooling, healthcare and peace, the higher the value; the fewer opportunities there are, the lower the value.

The external value of nationalities represents the extent to which holders of a particular nationality can genuinely enjoy the benefits of a globalized world and an increasingly trans-national life. The more they are restrained by national borders, the less the value; the less noticeable the borders, the higher the value. While many opt for a life at home, for a substantial number of people building a new life somewhere else is a dream, a reality, or both. External value of nationality is calculated through four sub-elements: the diversity and weight of settlement freedom, and the diversity and weight of travel freedom. Diversity of settlement freedom considers the number of "full access" countries, i.e. countries where the holders of a given nationality can work, live and settle freely with either no or merely minimal formalities. Secondly, the weight of settlement freedom measures the aggregate value of these full access countries based on their economic strength and level of human development. All data on settlement freedom is based on extensive literature research and consultations with experts on free movement from all regions in the world, resulting in an unprecedented overview of global work and settlement opportunities outside one's country of nationality. Diversity and weight are likewise gauged for Travel Freedom, i.e. the countries that a holder of a particular nationality can visit for tourist or business purposes without having to obtain a visa in advance. For this purpose, the QNI uses the Henley & Partners Visa Restrictions Index in conjunction with data from the International Air Transport Association (IATA), which manages the largest and most accurate database on worldwide visa regimes.

The incorporation of both Settlement Freedom and Travel Freedom is extremely important. In regulating the access of foreigners to their territories, countries make a distinction between travel access for tourist or business purposes, which is usually limited to a couple of months, and settlement access, which allows foreigners to work and stay for a longer period of time. If you are granted settlement access to a country, you are in many respects given "home treatment". This makes settlement access fundamentally different from travel access for tourist or business purposes, which is not associated with such privileges. The QNI takes into account both aspects because they measure distinct – albeit equally important – aspects of freedom: on the one hand, the freedom to travel widely without prior visa applications and visit a multitude of fascinating places. On the other hand, the freedom to settle yourself somewhere else on a longer term and be able to build a new life there.

Thus, the combination of internal and external value of nationality creates a realistic perspective on all the different types of chances and constraints we encounter in an ever globalized world, where borders between nation states increasingly fade, yet continue to affect our options to travel and settle abroad in search of new endeavors, inspiring chances and successful accomplishments. The QNI General Ranking presents nationalities in four categories: Very High Quality, High Quality, Medium Quality and Low Quality nationalities.

Very high quality	High quality	Medium quality	Low quality

In addition to the QNI General Ranking, which takes into account all seven sub-elements mentioned above, the QNI also offers three separate rankings specifically based on the external value of nationalities. The reason for these rankings is simply that the various sub-elements have intrinsic value in themselves – you may think, for example, of the importance of being able to travel widely without requiring prior visa applications. The table opposite illustrates the QNI General Ranking, External Value of Nationality Ranking, Settlement Freedom Ranking and Travel Freedom Ranking. For each ranking, the weight of the applicable sub-elements is indicated. A more extensive on the build-up of the rankings can be found in Section V below.

QNI General Ranking

1 Human development: 15%
2 Economic strength: 15%
3 Peace and stability: 10%
4 Diversity of settlement freedom: 15%
5 Weight of settlement freedom: 15%
6 Diversity of travel freedom: 15%
7 Weight of travel freedom: 15%

External Value of Nationality Ranking

1 Diversity of settlement freedom: 25%
2 Weight of settlement freedom: 25%
3 Diversity of travel freedom: 25%
4 Weight of travel freedom: 25%

Settlement Freedom Ranking

1 Diversity of settlement freedom: 50%
2 Weight of settlement freedom: 50%

Travel Freedom Ranking

1 Diversity of travel freedom: 50%
2 Weight of travel freedom: 50%

The rest of this chapter further expands the approach, sources and methodology of the QNI. Section II outlines the nationalities and similar legal statuses that are included in the QNI – and those that are not. Section III concisely describes the methodology as regards the time of measurement for each annual edition of the QNI. In Section IV, the various sub-elements of the QNI and their sources are examined in detail. Section V, lastly, deals with the way in which the QNI commeasures these sub-elements and how the QNI rankings are constructed. A more in-depth explanation of the general methodology and specific deviations can be found in the Annexes.

2 Nationalities included in the QNI

The QNI defines "Nationalities" as inheritable legal statuses of attachment to a public authority – usually a state – which entitle the holder to a passport or a passport-like travel document. The overwhelming majority of nationalities worldwide are ranked in this Index. These
include practically all United Nations Member States plus Kosovo, the Palestinian Territory,
Taiwan, Hong Kong and Macao. Only nationalities for which no reliable data on any of the
sub-elements is available are excluded. In addition, the following statuses are ranked as well:

• The legal status of non-citizens of Latvia

• Citizenship of the EU

Non-citizens of Latvia

The legal status of non-citizens of Latvia is granted to former nationals of the Soviet Union belonging to ethnic minorities who were living
in Latvia when the Soviet Union collapsed and do not possess Latvian
nationality nor that of any other country. Children of the holders of
the non-citizen Latvian status can inherit it, which makes it a real
nationality within the meaning of QNI, notwithstanding the fact that
the bearers, not being Latvian citizens, are unquestionably stateless
in the eyes of international law.

Citizens of the European Union

The EU provides the nationals of its 28 Member States with a formal citizenship status that
complements their national-level statuses. EU citizenship grants its holders the genuine freedom to pursue their own choices in terms of where they want to live and work within the Member
States of the EU. In this respect, it is reminiscent of traditional nationalities. Nevertheless, EU
citizenship is in many respects a peculiar concept. It is fully parasitic upon the nationalities of
the Member States – one cannot become an EU citizen unless one holds an EU Member States'
nationality. Furthermore, EU citizenship is not embodied in a passport or equivalent travel document: EU citizens must use their national passport to be able to enjoy its value. EU national
passports, however, are standardized in many respects.[1] Given the standardization and prohi-
bition of discrimination on the basis of the nationalities of the 28 Member States, EU citizenship
behaves, in many respects, like any other nationality considered for the purposes of this index.

---

1   See Council Regulation (EC) No 2252/2004 of 13 December 2004 on standards for security features and biomet-
    rics in passports and travel documents issued by Member States [2004] OJ L385/1

Thus EU citizenship is much like an extra perk that particular nationalities grant their holders, and which is not embodied in an independent physical document of a single design, although it clearly is a single legal status. The inherently particular nature of EU citizenship building on the nationalities of 28 Member States of the EU implies that the value of being an EU citizen is not absolute – it depends on the nationality one has. Therefore, for the purposes of the QNI, EU citizenship is a legal fiction whose value is based on the values of its constituent nationalities. This enables us to measure the average value of being an EU citizen. The value of EU citizenship is calculated as follows:

- In calculating EU citizenship's economic strength, the economic strength of its Member States are aggregated

- For the human development, peace and stability, diversity of travel freedom and weight of travel freedom, the value of EU citizenship is calculated by the average of its constituting nationalities. For example, the human development score of EU citizenship is equal to the average level of human development in the EU as expressed by the average score on the HDI of its current 28 Member States

- For the diversity and the weight of settlement freedom only settlement outside the EU is counted, to ensure that the EU nationality does not receive an undue advantage in the index. In 2015 the absolute majority of EU citizens can freely settle in three countries: Iceland, Norway and Switzerland.

Statuses and documents excluded from the index as failing to meet the criteria of a nationality

Excluded from the QNI are non-inheritable and/or idiosyncratic legal statuses and the travel documents that give them expression, which do not correlate to a possession of a real nationality in a legal sense commonly recognized in international law. Also fantasy passports and quasi-nationalities of *de facto* or *de jure* non-existent countries are excluded. Consequently, excluded are, *inter alia*:

- All refugee travel documents

- Certificates of identity that can be granted by States to stateless persons or refugees who cannot obtain a valid passport from their State of nationality

- UN Laissez-Passer. This document is granted to staff of the UN and specific international organizations and can be used as a valid travel document on official missions

- All other Laissez-Passer documents

- 1954 Convention travel documents, which can be granted to stateless persons pursuant to the 1954 Convention Relating to the Status of Stateless Persons

- Passport of the Sovereign Military Order of Malta. This travel document is granted to officials of the Sovereign Military Order of Malta, a Roman Catholic religious order and does not correspond to a nationality in international law, notwithstanding the international legal personality of the order

  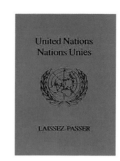

- Nationalities and corresponding passports of *de facto* existing countries that have particularly limited recognition, for example the nationalities of Abkhazia, Nagorno-Karabakh, South Ossetia, Transnistria, or the "Turkish Republic of Northern Cyprus". These countries are generally not recognized internationally or only by a handful of other States. Thus their passports do not provide travel and/or settlement opportunities, nor is sufficiently reliable information on their economic strength, peace and stability and human development available

- Nationalities and passports issued in the name of the occupied territories with no recognized statehood, like Western Sahara

- Passports corresponding to sub-national statuses of belonging, such as the passport of the Faroe Islands, which, as long as it corresponds to the Danish nationality is to be treated as Danish for the purposes of this index

- Camouflage and fantasy passports of *de facto* and also *de jure* non-existent countries: passports issued in the name of a non-existing country, which, therefore, cannot testify to the possession of any existing nationality. Camouflage passports are mostly used for false identification and/or criminal activities, and are generally issued under the name of a country no longer in existence, for example:

- British West Indies
- British Honduras (now Belize)
- Bophuthatswana (now part of South Africa)
- Burma or Birma (now Myanmar)
- Ceylon (now Sri Lanka)
- Ciskei (now part of South Africa)
- Dahomey (now Benin)
- Dutch Guiana (now Suriname)
- Eastern Samoa (now American Samoa)
- Western Samoa (now Samoa)

- Federal Republic of Yugoslavia
- Gilbert Islands (now Kiribati)
- Netherlands Guiana (now Suriname)
- New Grenada
- Netherlands West Indies (now Netherlands Antilles - part of NL sovereign territory)
- Netherlands East Indies (now Indonesia)
- New Hebrides (now Vanuatu)
- Rhodesia (now Zimbabwe)
- Republic of Zanzibar (now belongs to Tanzania)

- Spanish Guiana (now Equatorial Guinea)
- Sealand
- South Vietnam (now Vietnam)
- St. Christopher and Nevis (now St. Kitts and Nevis)
- Transkei (now part of South Africa)

- USSR (now divided into successor States)
- Windward Islands (now Dominica, St. Lucia, St. Vincent and the Grenadines)
- Zaire (now the Democratic Republic of Congo)[2]

Fantasy passports are used for a variety of purposes, but mostly for making political statements. Some prominent examples:[3]

- World Service Authority passport
- Aboriginal Free State passport
- *Celtic Druidic* ID / *Carte d'identité Celtique Druidique* / *Carta d'identità celtica druidica/ Keltisch-Druidischer Ausweis*
- "Hare Krishna Sect" (Krishna-Consciousness) passport
- "*Etats et la dynastie des carolingiens berniciens*" passport

---

2   This non-exhaustive list is derived from the European Union's "Information concerning the non-exhaustive list of known fantasy and camouflage passports, as stipulated by article 6 of the decision no 1105/2011/eu (to which a visa may not be affixed) based of information received from the member states until 18.08.2015"

3   A more comprehensive list can be found in the European Union's "Information concerning the non-exhaustive list of known fantasy and camouflage passports, as stipulated by article 6 of the decision no 1105/2011/eu (to which a visa may not be affixed) based of information received from the member states until 18.08.2015"

Nationalities excluded from the QNI due to lack of data

The following nationalities have been excluded from the QNI because there is no HDI data available for their issuing country:

- North Korea (Democratic People's Republic of Korea)
- Marshall Islands
- Nauru
- Somalia
- South Sudan
- Tuvalu
- Vatican City

The following nationalities have been excluded because their issuing countries are not included in the GPI, nor can a reliable estimation be made:

- Fiji

- Kiribati

- Federated States of Micronesia

- Independent State of Samoa

- Solomon Islands

- Tonga

- Vanuatu

3   Time of measurement

The annual QNI represents the status quo on 1 May of that year. This will ensure that the QNI is based on the latest and most up-to-date data available on that date. Where data as is current on 1 May is not available, the most recent data available is used. Such deviations from the use of current data are listed in Annexes.

For example, the QNI 2015 is based on the 2014 HDI, the most recent GDP and NRR data, the 2014 Global Peace Index, and tourist and business visa regimes as of 1 May 2015.

Tourist and business visa regime changes after 1 May are integrated in the QNI of the subsequent year.

General exception: Settlement Freedom

As regards Settlement Freedom, all data is based on the status quo on 31 December of the preceding year. Hence, QNI 2015 for example is based on the settlement access regimes as of 31 December 2014. Global settlement freedom is collected through analysis of legal regimes worldwide, secondary literature and expert consultation. Because of the scale of necessary research and the absence of comprehensive databases, Settlement Freedom requires this earlier time of measurement.

4 Elements and sources of the QNI

Human Development

The basic level of development associated with a nationality provides a rough prophecy for the average person's life prospects. The disparities between the average life expectancy, level of education and general welfare of sub-Saharan nationals and Western European nationals dramatically illustrate this regrettable fact. Therefore, the importance of the level of human development for the quality of a nationality requires little elaboration; the overwhelming majority of people spend most of their lives in their home country, and are profoundly affected by the basic level of its development. The most essential way in which our nationalities shape our future is the circumstances in which they force us to grow up and develop ourselves. Whether we achieve success or wealth, whether we live a prosperous and healthy life, and whether we can become the person we want to be, or know what one can want to be, is largely dependent on the degree of human development of the territory in which we find ourselves by birth. Also in a globalized world, human development in the country of origin will always substantially affect our life prospects, including the ability to become a global citizen later in life.

The QNI derives the degree of human development from the United Nations Development Programme Human Development Index (HDI), which is today's most authoritative ranking of basic human development. The HDI is an annual index based on the idea that the development of a country is not reflected in its economic strength or growth per se, but in its people and their capabilities. Its methodology is designed by the Pakistani economist Mahbub ul Haq together with a team of economists including Nobel Laureate Amartya Sen, in order to evaluate non-economic development in the simplest possible manner so as to make it intelligible for a wide audience. The index measures three dimensions of human development: health, education and standard of living:

- Health is measured by life expectancy at birth, with a minimum value of 20 years and maximum of 85 years
- Education is assessed by the mean of the number of years of schooling for adults aged 25 years and the expected years of schooling for children of school entering age
- Standard of living is measured by gross national income per capita

HDI scores do not reflect inequalities, poverty, human security, empowerment, or other factors directly, although the factors obviously exert influence on the levels of health, education and standard of living indirectly.

HDI scores are directly mirrored in the Human Development component of the QNI: the higher the country's score on the HDI, the higher the Human Development score of the corresponding nationality. Some countries are not included in the HDI, while their nationalities have been evaluated in the QNI because reasonable estimations could be made. A list of these nationalities is available in the Annexes.

Human Development Index (HDI)

Health	Education	Standard of Living
Measured by life expectancy at birth, with a minimum value of 20 years and maximum value of 85 years	Assessed by the mean of the number of years of schooling for adults aged 25 years and the expected years of schooling for children of school entering	Measured by gross national income per capita

Economic Strength

The value of nationality is greatly influenced by the economic strength of the country that grants the status. Economic strength is all about scale: stronger economies offer more opportunities in private and professional life, creating more value for their nationals. We measure economic strength by Gross Domestic Product (GDP), which is defined by the World Bank as the "sum of gross value added by all resident producers in the economy plus any product taxes and minus any subsidies not included in the value of the products". The larger the country is economically, the stronger its economic strength is and hence, the higher the score is of the corresponding nationality.

As we have seen above, the HDI takes into account welfare and standard of living by measuring GDP per capita. Why then include economic strength in GDP separately as well?

The reason is simple: welfare and general development are surely quintessential for a prosperous life, but we equally value scale of opportunity. Being a national of the US, for example, enables someone to pursue endless opportunities without crossing national borders. This makes US nationality more valuable in comparison to the nationality of, for example, Hong Kong, even though they have a comparable GDP per capita. Including GDP ensures that nationalities of larger countries are valued higher than economically comparable but smaller countries, reflecting the greater number of life chances they offer.

Economic strength is measured by a country's share of world GDP at Purchasing Power Parity (PPP), excluding rents from the exploitation of natural resources – or so-called Natural Resources Rents (NRR).

Applying PPP converts countries' GDP into international dollars. An international dollar possesses the same purchasing power as a US dollar has in the US. Such conversion makes economies more comparable because the GDP figures reflect the actual size of the economy from a consumer perspective. By using PPP GDP, the QNI gives a more realistic perspective on the economic strength of nationalities for the purpose of valuing their quality. Instead of measuring the formal scale of economies without due regard to genuine purchasing power, the QNI measures the real and comparable opportunities that nationalities offer.

NRR is the sum of oil rents, natural gas rents, coal rents (hard and soft), mineral rents, and forest rents. NRR is excluded from the measurement of economic strength to avoid substantial distortion of the value of some nationalities. While economic strength is principally intended to reflect all economic opportunities granted to holders of a nationality, NRR is not suitable to reflect the genuine scale of a country that works to the benefit of its nationals. Some African and Middle Eastern countries, for example, have relatively large economies that are substantially dependent on NRR. This distorts the values of their nationalities: their economic strength is not reflected in the scale of economic and social opportunities that their nationals enjoy. Including NRR, for example, gives Algeria and Iraq a relatively high score, which in light of the assets of their nationalities would be unwarranted.

Depending on the nationality concerned, whether or not NRR is included in measuring Economic Strength can make a substantial difference. Most European economies rely little on NRR, such as France (0.12% of GDP), Germany (0.15% of GDP) and Poland (1.40% of GDP), or have no appreciable NRR are at all, such as Monaco and San Marino. The Economic Strength of their nationalities in terms of the scale of economic opportunities they offer is practically equal to their PPP GDP.

By contrast, other countries rely substantially on NRR, such as Norway (10.93% of PPP GDP), Suriname (26.78% of GDP), or Saudi Arabia (46.19% of GDP). By measuring only the GDP generated by economic activity other than NRR in those countries, the scale of economic

opportunities of their nationalities becomes more commensurable to the scale of economic opportunities of nationalities such as those of France and Germany.

The PPP GDP data is collected from the International Monetary Fund (IMF). For some countries, no (or not all) PPP GDP is available in the IMF database. Where no sufficiently recent and/or reliable PPP GDP data could be used, (non PPP) GDP data from the World Bank is applied. Since the countries for which no PPP GDP is available generally have an extremely small-scale economy, the use of nominal GDP figures is highly unlikely to have affected their ranking. A list of countries for which non-PPP GDP data was used can be found in the Annexes.

NRR in percentage of GDP is also collected from the World Bank.

Peace and Stability

The importance of a peaceful, stable and safe environment cannot be overestimated. A peaceful society likely fosters human development, welfare and happiness more than anything else. Conversely, war and violence can dramatically affect the fate of having a particular nationality, in particular for nationalities that grant their holders few to no global opportunities. The current migrant crisis in the Middle East is only the most recent example of the fact that the difficulty or virtual impossibility to escape your country of nationality can result in immense tragedies. Peace and Stability is especially important therefore, in particular for nationalities that offer few global opportunities.

For measuring Peace and Stability, the QNI uses figures from the annual GPI published by the Institute for Economics and Peace. The GPI is an annual ranking that measures the peacefulness, stability and harmony of countries by looking at 23 indicators of peace, divided into three domains: ongoing domestic and international conflict, the level of harmony within a nation and the degree of militarization:

- Ongoing domestic and international conflict, which measures the role, intensity and duration of countries in internal and external conflicts. Six indicators are used, including the number of deaths from organized conflict and the relations with neighboring countries
- The level of harmony within a nation, evaluating 10 indicators of a safe and secure society including low crime rates, minimal terrorist activity, the number of refugees as a percentage of the population, and a stable political scene
- Degree of militarization, which applies seven indicators such as military expenditure as a percentage of GDP, nuclear and heavy weapons capabilities and the ease of access to small arms

The GPI makes a distinction between internal and external peace, both of which are measured separately using the weighted values of all indicators. Internal peace refers to the level of peace within a country's borders, which includes domestic conflict, security, access to small arms, and so on. Conversely, external peace measures the level of peace of a country outside its own borders, for which inter alia relations with neighboring countries and participation in peacekeeping missions are relevant. The GPI ranking is the combination of internal peace (counting for 60%) and external peace (counting for 40%).

GPI scores are directly converted to Peace and Stability scores for the QNI. Therefore, the better a country scores on the GPI, the higher the Peace and Stability score of the corresponding nationality is.

Some countries are not included in the GPI, while their nationalities have been evaluated in the QNI because reasonable estimations are available based on the average scores of surrounding countries or the region. A list of these nationalities and the methodology of calculating a reasonable estimation can be found in the Annexes.

Diversity of Settlement Freedom

The QNI recognizes the unfortunate reality that nationality significantly affects our opportunities, welfare and life chances, despite the fact that no one is ever capable of choosing the nationality of origin. The contrast between the immense number of different cultures, lifestyles and living environments in the world and the corresponding limitations of our country of origin is nothing but regrettable. Therefore, the freedom to settle elsewhere outside one's own country of nationality is considered a profound asset that allows us to escape the box in which we were born. Precisely because the country of nationality by definition can only give us merely limited options compared with the vastness of the totality of the world outside national borders – a truth applicable to any nationality, from Canada to

Swaziland, no matter how large and powerful the country the nationality is associated with is – the extent to which a nationality provides a rainbow of additional opportunities by virtue of granting the ability to settle and work abroad can give this nationality either immense or negligible value. Even for those who will never swap countries, knowing that they are virtually unconditionally welcome to join another society with its

opportunities and culture will be an empowering thought, while others will actually opt to actively use this right by either moving or choosing to live in several countries at the same time. The number of such people is growing.

Thus the QNI includes diversity of settlement freedom as an inherent part of the quality of nationalities. Consequently, the number of full-access countries is measured. Full-access countries are countries where the holder of a particular nationality can freely work and live following either none or only minimal immigration requirements. Regardless of the quality of the countries outside of your country of nationality in which you can freely settle, a diverse palette of settlement options possesses inherent value for nationality. The more countries giving full-access settlement to the holder of a nationality, the higher that nationality's score is on Diversity of Settlement Freedom.

Nationals of the majority of EU Member States have full-access to the rest of the EU, EEA and Switzerland. Accordingly, in 2015 the nationalities of EU Member States are granted settlement freedom to 29 or 30 countries – the difference is mostly due to the access policy for Croatian nationality and to Croatia. In comparison, the settlement freedom of non-EU nationalities is far more limited. For

example, nationals of Belarus can settle freely in five other countries: Armenia, Russia, Kyrgyzstan, Kazakhstan and Georgia. The nationality of the Marshall Islands gives full-access to the Federated States of Micronesia, Palau and the US.

The inclusion of Diversity of Settlement Freedom illustrates the QNI's unique nature in displaying the quality of nationalities, as all other rankings on quality of life most broadly perceived focus only on the internal aspects of countries. No analogous source exists on the settlement freedom that nationalities grant their holders. For the first time, accordingly, the QNI provides an exclusive overview of the diversity of global life chances.

The freedom to settle abroad is constrained throughout the world by numerous limitations – you can think of access to social benefits, health care insurance and the labor market. Therefore, "full-access" must be interpreted somewhat loosely because there are virtually no countries in which foreigners are completely assimilated without any conditions. For measuring Diversity of Settlement Freedom, settlement in a particular country is considered possible if:

- An adult holder of a nationality is allowed to work or stay by independent means in another country for at least 360 days without having to obtain a visa or with visa on arrival
- Permission to work in that country is either not required or virtually automatic

In other words, settlement freedom does not entail that the holder of a nationality is given carte blanche to settle in a different country. What this sub-element primarily measures are the options to either work somewhere else or stay there provided you can maintain yourself independently. Further, all the following aspects are not considered in determining the freedom to settle in another country:

- Entitlement to public pension systems
- Entitlement to health care
- Entitlement to social security benefits
- Allowance to family members to join the person in question
- Specific skill qualifications that are required to perform certain professions, particularly of a qualitative nature, e.g., bar qualifications to practice as lawyer, medical qualifications to practice as a doctor, or construction worker qualifications

Although no settlement freedom is unlimited, by focusing on the genuine possibility to work or live independently in a different country, the QNI is able to measure the diversity of settlement freedom in a realistic and accurate manner. Notwithstanding constraints or difficulties you may confront when making use of your settlement freedom as defined in the QNI, the ability to access other countries and exploit the life chances given there is genuine and profoundly valuable.

Since the QNI measures the quality of nationalities, it does not take into account any settlement freedom, which is not uniquely based on nationality as such, but also on other factors, such as being in possession of a higher education diploma, as is the case in CARICOM, for instance.

Data on the diversity of settlement freedom is gathered through extensive literature research on the legal requirements on settlement throughout the world. Research on the formal legal requirements is complemented with consultations with experts in all regions of the world. This ensures that only real and genuine settlement freedom is taken into account, and paper tigers or sham legal freedoms are discarded. As no antecedent on this topic exists, the QNI is the only source on global settlement freedom worldwide.

Weight of Settlement Freedom

While diversity of settlement freedom provides intrinsic value to boost freedom and life chances, clearly not all destinations are equal: being allowed to work in Canada is more valuable than being allowed to work in Bulgaria or Côte d'Ivoire. In other words, diversity is highly important, but it is not the Holy Grail in itself.

For example, from 2015 Russians are allowed to settle in four countries (Armenia, Belarus, Kyrgyzstan and Kazakhstan). By contrast, people from the Federated States of Micronesia can settle in three countries: the US, Palau and the Marshall Islands. Despite having access to fewer countries, however, it is absolutely clear that a Micronesian passport has more value in terms of settlement freedom than a Russian passport. After all, full-access to the US in itself provides for infinitely more economic opportunities than Armenia, Belarus, Kyrgyzstan and Kazakhstan combined, in addition to the US providing a higher level of human development.

Therefore, the QNI also includes measurement of the combined value of the countries that a nationality allows you to settle in. This Weight of Settlement Freedom value is composed of the sum of all such countries' weighted scores on Human Development and Economic Strength, which are each given 50% weight.

For example, in 2015 the French nationality allowed you to settle in 30 countries. The Weight of Settlement Freedom score of French nationality is calculated by the sum of the weighted scores of these 30 countries. Each country's weighted score is in turn calculated by the sum of its weighted score on Human Development (counting for 50%) and Economic Strength (counting for 50%).

Weight of Settlement Freedom combines the existing Human Development and Economic Strength with the QNI's research on the settlement opportunities for nationals worldwide. In this respect, this ranking gives a reliable overview of the global opportunities you have – if only potentially. The higher the level of human development and the scale of economic opportunity that a nationality allows you to pursue outside the issuing country's borders, the higher is that nationality's score on Weight of Settlement Freedom. By measuring the quality in terms of economic scale and opportunity and human development of all the possible settlements, the QNI adds an indispensable external component to the quality of life within one's country of origin.

Diversity of Travel Freedom

Diversity of Travel Freedom measures the number of tourist and business access countries the holder of a particular nationality can visit visa-free or with a visa on arrival for a short-term stay. Work or recourse to public funds is usually strictly prohibited.

Visa restrictions play an important role in controlling the possibilities for (foreign) nationals to travel freely across borders. Almost all countries now require visas from certain non-nationals who wish to enter (or leave) their territory. A visa allows you to travel to the destination country as far as the port of entry (airport, seaport or land border crossing) and ask the immigration officer to allow you to enter the country. In most countries the immigration officer usually also decides how long you can stay for any particular visit. In most countries, a tourist and business access visa allows you to stay in the country between one and three months.

Diversity of Travel Freedom is a valuable aspect of the quality of nationalities. It gauges the extent to which holders of a particular nationality can freely travel without extensive administrative hassles and time-consuming preparation. In today's world, where the border control of any country is rarely more than 24 hours away irrespective of your current location, the freedom to travel  is a wonderful good, the fruits of which are experienced by many fortunate people. Nevertheless, visa applications cannot only be time-consuming: for holders of some nationalities they are actually unpredictable and at worst unlikely to be successful. In the cases of some nationalities, access to certain countries for tourist or business purposes is *de facto* impossible. Holders of Armenian passports intending to see Azerbaijan, or Israelis intending to do business in some Arab countries are the cases in point. Even in a globalized world where virtually any place on Earth can be reached in the blink of an eye, visa restrictions pose serious constraints, and unfortunately for some nationalities this constraint is much more serious than for others.

In 2015 a British or German passport, for example, allowed you to visit no fewer than 174 countries visa-free or by visa on arrival, while in comparison an Iranian passport only gives such access to 40 countries. Large countries do not necessarily provide substantial travel freedom; an Indian passport for example only grants visa-free or visa on arrival access to 52 countries and is easily

surpassed by countries like Bulgaria, with visa-free or visa on arrival access to 149 countries.

For measuring Diversity of Travel Freedom, the Henley & Partners Visa Restrictions Index (HVRI) is used. This Index is a global ranking of countries according to the travel freedom that their nationals enjoy. The ranking is based on the number of destinations that nationals of countries have short-term tourist or business access to without having to obtain a visa and is produced by Henley & Partners in cooperation with the International Air Transport Association (IATA), which is the trade association of the overwhelming majority of airlines. IATA maintains IATA Timatic, the world's largest and most reliable database of travel information.

Countries are listed according to the numbers of destinations to which visa-free or visa on arrival tourist and business access is possible. Hence, the highest score is achieved by the nationalities of Finland, Germany, Sweden, the UK and the US, who can all access 174 destinations and are ranked in 1st position. For the QNI, the country scores in the HVRI are directly transposed to the corresponding nationality. The more destinations a nationality allows you to visit for tourist or business purposes without prior visa application, the higher is that nationality's value in terms of Diversity of Travel Freedom.

In measuring travel freedom, the HVRI takes into account the possible destinations for a large number of nationalities. There are 219 destinations in total. The number of nationalities evaluated is 199. These are the nationalities of the 193 UN Member States, Taiwan, Kosovo, Palestinian Territory, Vatican City, Hong Kong (SAR China) and Macao (SAR China).

Some territories count as a destination but are not considered as a nationality. These are territories which enforce their own entry requirements, but are governed by other countries and people originating from these territories only hold passports issued by the governing country. The following territories are considered as destinations for the travel freedom part of this index but not nationalities:

• Territories dependent on the UK: Anguilla, Bermuda, Cayman Islands, Falkland Islands, Gibraltar, Montserrat, Turks and Caicos Islands, Virgin Islands (British) [4]

---

4   The majority of those originating from these territories hold, besides other statuses, also a full British citizenship.

- Territories dependent on Australia: Norfolk Island

- Territories associated with New Zealand: Cook Islands, Niue

- Territories under administration of the US: Guam, Northern Mariana Islands, Puerto Rico, Samoa (American), Virgin Islands (US)

- Territories under administration of the Kingdom of the Netherlands: Aruba, Bonaire, St. Eustatius, Saba, Curaçao and St. Maarten

- Territories dependent on France in the Caribbean as well as in the Atlantic, Indian and Pacific Oceans

Weight of Travel Freedom

Also for Travel Freedom, the actual quality of the countries and territories, which a particular nationality allows you to visit visa-free or with a visa on arrival is considered having equal value as the diversity of possible travel destinations. Being able to travel to many countries is in itself a splendid good, but surely some countries are more valuable and are more worth a visit than others. For most people, being able to travel freely to the UK or France will be more valuable than having no visa obligation for Kiribati or Syria.

For example, in 2015 a Russian passport gave visa-free or visa on arrival tourist and business access to 100 countries. None of these 100 destinations, however, are first world countries: prior visa application is necessary for, amongst others, the US, EU countries, Australia, Japan and Canada. Its Weight of Travel Freedom is therefore relatively low with a score of 41.31. By contrast, a passport of the Republic of Moldova gave visa-free or visa on arrival tourist and business access to 89 countries, but this includes countries of the Schengen area. As a result, its Weight of Travel Freedom score is 43.46; slightly higher than Russian nationality despite the lower number of destinations.

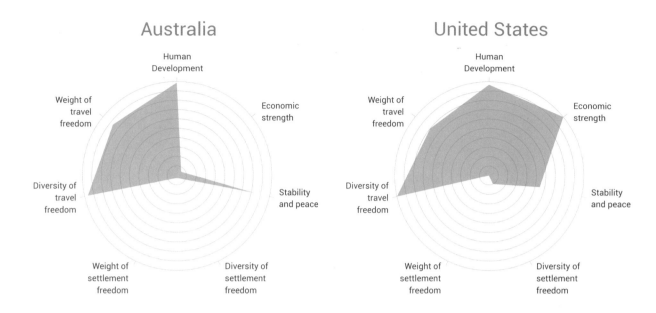

Australia

United States

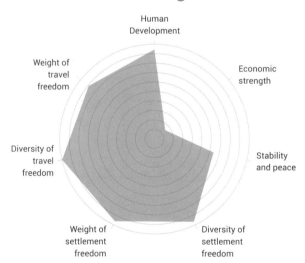

Canada

United Kingdom

Therefore, the QNI measures the Weight of Travel Freedom in addition to its diversity and applies the same principles that are applied for Weight of Settlement Freedom: the combined value of all countries allowing visa-free or visa on arrival tourist and business access to the holders of a nationality is composed of the sum of all these countries' weighted scores on Human Development (counting for 50%) and Economic Strength (counting for 50%)

As mentioned above, the exact countries that a particular nationality allows its holders to visit visa-free or by visa on arrival is not publicly available. The Weight of Settlement Freedom values are calculated by IATA specifically for the QNI, using the abovementioned formula and based on visa regimes as of 1 May 2015. This allows the QNI to provide a unique overview of the aggregate value of the destinations we can easily reach for holidays or work.

Some of the countries which can be visited visa-free or by visa on arrival do not feature in the QNI because there is no data available on Human Development and/or Peace and Stability. There are also countries that are excluded because they lack own nationality, despite the existence of own immigration controls (e.g. Aruba, New Caledonia and American Samoa). Notwithstanding their own absence in the QNI, these countries and territories have been ascribed a minimal weighted score of 0.1. This ensures that the possibility to visit these countries visa-free does not go unnoticed. All the territories enforcing their own border controls which are assigned such a symbolic weight are listed in the Annex.

5   Measurement and rankings of the QNI

The QNI offers four rankings that measure various combinations of the sub-elements: the QNI General Ranking, which comprises all seven sub-elements described above; the External Value of Nationality Ranking, based on the four sub-elements measuring external value of nationalities; the Settlement Freedom Ranking, which measures the diversity and weight of settlement freedom specifically; and the Travel Freedom Ranking, which is concerned with the diversity and weight of travel freedom. The QNI General Ranking might be interesting for everyone who would like to know how their nationality performs in comparison to others, and is interested in the local, regional and global opportunities granted by their nationality. The three rankings based on the external value of nationality might appeal to particular people: travel-addicts will be especially interested in the diversity and weight of travel freedom. Cosmopolitans and chronically restless souls will also find the diversity and weight of settlement freedom of interest. All in all, the four QNI rankings give a comprehensive indication of the value, constraints and freedom of having a particular nationality. Thus, the QNI is meant for everyone who is eager to look beyond the borders of their home country and is concerned with global mobility, life chances and limitations.

General Ranking

The QNI General Ranking ranks the nationalities' value most broadly interpreted, including internal opportunities, welfare and life prospects, as well as the freedom to travel and settle throughout the world. In the most comprehensive manner possible, the QNI General Ranking can be said to gauge quality of life in a globalized world.

The QNI General Ranking will accordingly rank nationalities on a scale from 0% to 100%. Scores will be rounded to one decimal place. The following weights are attributed to the separate sub-elements:

QNI General Ranking

1   Human development: 15%
2   Economic strength: 15%
3   Peace and stability: 10%
4   Diversity of settlement freedom: 15%
5   Weight of settlement freedom: 15%
6   Diversity of travel freedom: 15%
7   Weight of travel freedom: 15%

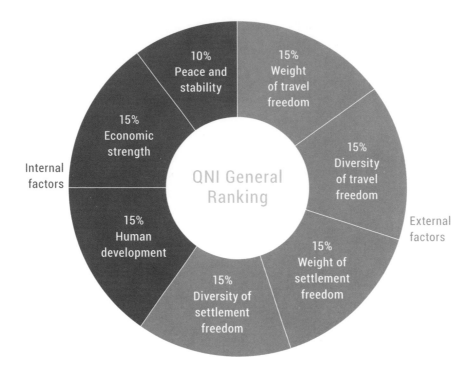

The QNI General Ranking comprises internal value (40%) and external value (60%) of nationality. Indeed, the basic premise of the QNI is that quality of life must be measured with due regard to the decreasing – albeit still ever present – relevance of borders and nation states in the lives of the global citizens. For this reason, substantial weight is attributed to the external value of nationalities. As mentioned above, diversity and weight are equally relevant in this regard, since both are fundamental indicators of the quality of global life chances.

As regards the internal value of nationalities, Peace and Stability is given lower weight than Human Development and Economic Strength for multiple reasons. In the first place it is highly volatile. While the overwhelming majority of people will keep their nationalities for life, the peacefulness of many regions is regrettably far less stable. Furthermore, while Human Development and Economic Strength specifically measure the performance of the country granting nationality and thereby primary aspects of the quality of the corresponding nationality, Peace and Stability is not as directly connected to nationality as such. War and insecurity are surely terrible influences on the quality of life, but they are not primary features of nationality and affect the quality of nationality more indirectly. Lastly, elements of peace and stability are also reflected in the measurement of human development and economic strength. While neither GDP measurements nor the Human Development Index takes peacefulness into account directly, it is beyond doubt that a more peaceful and stable society generally results in a more prosperous economy offering more life chances, and is more likely to have a higher level of wealth, education and health and welfare in general.

The sub-elements of the QNI are the normalized scores of the nationalities. Data from the various sources is normalized by transforming the results to a scale that corresponds with the weight that is given to particular sub-element (10% for Peace and Stability and 15% for all other sub-elements). Each nationality is thus awarded a score based on its relative performance vis-à-vis the other nationalities.

For Peace and Stability, the GPI ranking is transformed to a scale from 0 to 10. The nationality granted by the safest country receives a full score of 10%. All other nationalities receive a score between 0 and 10 based on their GPI score in relation to the most peaceful country. This means that the nationality of country that according to the GPI is twice less peaceful as the most peaceful country will receive a score of 5%, nationality of a country which is five times less peaceful will receive 2%, and so on.

For example, in 2015 the world's most peaceful country according to the GPI was Denmark with a score of 1.14. The Danish nationality's QNI Peace and Stability score is accordingly a full score of 10%. Germany received a GPI score of 1.403. As the GPI applies a linear scale on which the lower the score, the more peaceful the country, German nationality is given a QNI Peace and

Stability score of 1.14 (Denmark's GPI) divided by 1.403 (Germany's GPI) and multiplied by 10 (the full QNI Peace and Stability score) ≈ 8.13.

For all other sub-elements, nationalities are given a ranking on a scale from 0 to 15. The highest scoring nationality will always receive full 15%, while other nationalities are ranked proportionately.

For example, in 2015 the strongest economy was the US with 15.94% of world GDP (PPP) excluding NRR. US nationality is thus given a full 15% on Economic Strength. China contributed 15.58% of PPP world GDP excluding NRR. Chinese nationality consequently scores on economic strength as 15.58 divided by 15.4 and multiplied by 15 ≈ 14.66%.

Quality categories

The resulting QNI General Ranking presents all nationalities on a 0% to 100% scale. Moreover, nationalities are categorized in four tiers:

1   **Very high quality:** nationalities with a value of 50.0% and above
2   **High quality:** nationalities with a value of between 35.0% and 49.9%
3   **Medium quality:** nationalities with a value of between 20.0% and 34.9%
4   **Low quality:** nationalities with a value of 19.9% and less

External Value of Nationality Ranking

The External Value of Nationality Ranking gives a comprehensive overview of the various types of globalized opportunities that nationalities grant their holders. It is therefore based on the all sub-elements related to external value of nationality. This ranking reflects the degree to which each nationality grants its holders global possibilities and opportunities, taking into account both the diversity and weight of travel freedom and those of settlement freedom.

All persons whose horizon lies beyond their national border, both regarding travel and settlement abroad, will find this ranking crucial for the assessment of the comparative instrumental worth of world nationalities. The External Value of Nationality Ranking is intended to present nationalities' values is the core added value of QNI: its departure from the basic premise held by the absolute majority of other rankings that only countries matter, not nationalities *per se*. Whereas internal value of nationality is quintessential for the majority of people who will probably spend most of their lives in their country of origin, it is not necessarily relevant for persons who consider the world their home, and are eager to live and work wherever fate brings them.

The External Value of Nationality Ranking is based on a scale from 0% to 100%. The following weights are used, reflecting equal value for diversity and weight, as well as equal weight for settlement and travel freedom:

External Value of Nationality Ranking

1   Diversity of settlement freedom: 25%
2   Weight of settlement freedom: 25%
3   Diversity of travel freedom: 25%
4   Weight of travel freedom: 25%

The normalized scores for the External Value of Nationality Ranking are calculated using the same principles as the QNI General Ranking – only the weights attributed to the sub-elements differ so that each ranking is based on a 0%–100% scale. On each sub-element, the highest scoring nationality on the respective index is attributed a full score of 25%, the other nationalities receive a proportionate score.

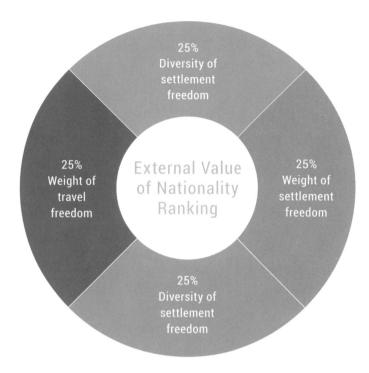

For example, in 2015, Czech, Danish, Estonian, Finnish, French, Irish, Liechtenstein, and Swedish nationality received the highest score on Diversity of Settlement Freedom. Holders of each of these nationalities could settle freely in 30 foreign countries. These nationalities are thus given a full score of 25% on the Diversity of Settlement Freedom component. Holders of Maltese nationality, for example, had settlement access to 29 countries. Maltese nationality is thus attributed a score of 29 divided by 30 and multiplied by 25 ≈ 24.17% on the Diversity of Settlement Freedom component. Scores for the other three components are calculated similarly.

Settlement Freedom Ranking

Following the basic premise of the QNI, the value of nationality depends significantly on the possibility to live and work elsewhere. Being a national of one of the EU Member States, for example, cannot be appreciated properly without giving due regard to the immense opportunities this gives you in the other Member States. Whether or not you intend to live part of your life abroad, the sole fact that you could do so gives your nationality more value in itself. In that respect, the quality of nationality of small EU Member States such as Belgium or the Netherlands is more comparable to US nationality than the vast difference in national economic scale suggests. The Settlement Freedom Ranking specifically focuses on the global opportunities and life chances nationalities can give you – reflecting individual freedom beyond borders.

For this purpose, the Settlement Freedom Ranking is composed of the diversity and weight of settlement freedom of nationalities. This ranking may appeal to a variety of persons – from those who are too restless to live and work in one and the same country for more than a few years to people working in business or government who are required to change location frequently. Most prominently rising in today's world, however, is the ever-growing group of location-independent entrepreneurs. Start-ups, commercial blogs, online marketing, to name just a few, are providing the basic means of income for an increasing number of people who are not tied to a specific country, and might be interested in knowing which possibilities their nationality grants them.

The Settlement Freedom Ranking is based on a scale from 0% to 100%. Diversity and weight are valued equally, resulting in the following weights:

Settlement Freedom Ranking

1   Diversity of settlement freedom: 50%
2   Weight of settlement freedom: 50%

The same principles are again applied to calculate the normalized scores of nationalities:

In 2015 holders of Czech, Danish, Estonian, Finnish, French, Irish, Liechtenstein and Swedish nationality could settle freely in 30 foreign countries. For the purpose of the Settlement Freedom Ranking, these nationalities are given a full score of 50%. Italian nationality, granting settlement access to 29 countries, is attributed a diversity of settlement freedom score of 29 divided by 30 and multiplied by 50 ≈ 48.33%. Non-EU nationalities invariably score much lower. For example, Liberian nationals have settlement access to 12 countries. Liberian nationality is attributed a score of 12 divided by 30 and multiplied by 50 = 20%.

In the same year, Liechtenstein nationality had the highest weight of settlement freedom. The aggregate value of all 30 countries to which a holder of Liechtenstein nationality has settlement access was 428.7. By comparison, Italian nationality received a weight of settlement freedom value of 413.0. Italian nationality receives thus a weight of settlement freedom score of 413.0 divided

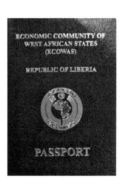

by 428.7 and multiplied by 50 ≈ 48.17. Liberian nationality, with weight of settlement freedom value 84.0, gets 84.0 divided by 428.7 and multiplied by 50 ≈ 9.80%.

The final score of Italian and Liberian nationality on the Settlement Freedom Ranking can now be calculated. As each sub-element has equal weight, the scores on the two sub-elements can simply be added up, resulting in a score of 48,33 + 48.17 = 96.50% for Italian nationality, equaling a shared 8th place in the ranking. Liberian nationality scores 20 + 9.80 = 29.80%, or a shared 14th place.

Travel Freedom Ranking

Practically all of us will be interested in our options to travel without the administrative hassles of prior visa applications. The Travel Freedom Ranking is based on both the diversity and weight of travel freedom, and describes our freedom to look beyond our borders and experience the world. By taking into account both diversity and weight, the Travel Freedom Ranking intends to combine the quantity and quality of travel destinations as accurately as possible. However, the weight of travel destinations is obviously only an indication of their quality – Human Development and Economic Strength are not necessarily sufficient or even necessary indicators of whether a destination is desirable. Surely, this will be dependent on each person's individual preferences, which might involve totally different considerations. Nevertheless, the QNI's methodology for calculating the weight of travel freedom does offer a general and rough indication of how the various destinations relate to each other. Traveling is indeed a beautiful opportunity to collect vivid experiences – and Human Development and

Economic Strength both reflect the number of opportunities you can encounter as well as the level of experiences you can collect.

Travel Freedom Ranking

1   Diversity of travel freedom: 50%
2   Weight of travel freedom: 50%

For example, Singaporean nationality gave visa-free or visa on arrival access for tourist or business purposes to 170 countries in 2015, while Finnish nationality had a shared first place on Diversity of Travel Freedom with 174 countries. Nationals of Costa Rica were able to travel freely to 125 countries.

Finnish nationality thus receives a full score of 50%, Singaporean nationality gets 170 divided by 174 and multiplied by 50 ≈ 48.85%. Costa Rican nationality's score is 125 divided by 174 and multiplied by 50 ≈ 35.92%.

The Weight of Travel Freedom, i.e. the aggregate weight of the 170 countries Singaporean nationals could visit, is 96.33%. The Weight of Travel Freedom of Finnish nationality is 90.40% and that of Costa Rican nationality 62.15%. As Singaporean nationality has the highest score on Weight of Travel Freedom, it receives a full score of 50%. Finnish nationality receives 90.40% divided by 96.33 and multiplied by 50 ≈ 46.92%, while Costa Rican nationality gets 32.26%.

The Travel Freedom Ranking scores can now be calculated. Singaporean nationality has a total score of 48.85% (Diversity of Travel Freedom) + 50 (Weight of Travel Freedom) = 98.85%, giving it 1st place. Finnish nationality has a total score of 50 + 46.92 = 96.92%, or a 3rd place. Costa Rican nationality has a total score of 35.92 + 32.26 = 68.18%, equaling a 54th place.

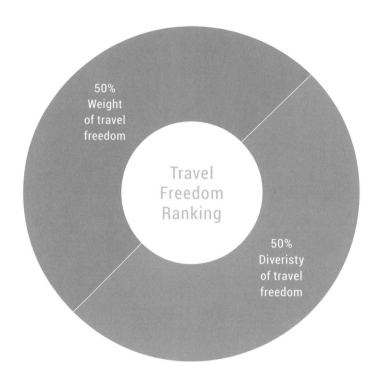

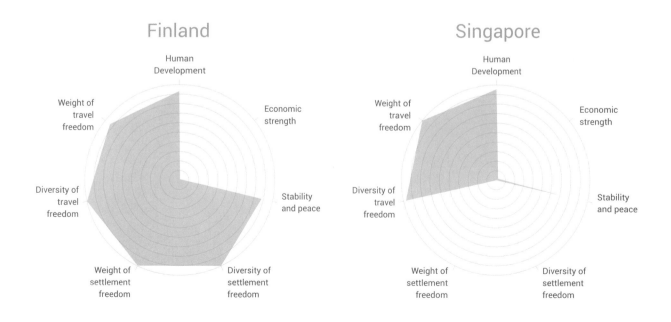

Part 2

A — NATIONALITIES OF THE
WORLD IN 2015

Nationalities of the world in 2015

In 2015, the quality of world nationalities was characterized by contrasting dynamics. While on average, the global quality of nationalities remained stable with a marginal improvement of 0.02% points, widely diverging movements are visible. As South America keeps a steady pace in economic integration, South American nationalities experienced a substantial increase in External and Overall Value. Meanwhile, regional destabilization in North Africa and the Middle East has adverse repercussions on quality. As a result, between 1 May 2014 and 1 May 2015, 88 nationalities lost value, 81 nationalities gained value and 16 nationalities remained stable. The global mean in 2015 was 38.70%, with German nationality ranking on top of the QNI General Ranking with 83.1%, and the nationality of the Democratic Republic of Congo at the bottom of the list with 14.3%.

The QNI distinguishes between four quality tiers. In 2015, 42 nationalities had a very high quality (above 50.0%), 30 nationalities scored a high quality (between 35.0% and 49.9%), 93 nationalities were in the medium quality tier (between 20.0% and 34.9%), and 21 nationalities had a low quality (below 20.0%).

Regions compared

Regional divergences in the quality of nationalities are manifest. The nationalities of Europe and North America outperform the global mean by a wide margin, with means of 62.79% (Europe), and 58.1% (North America). The EU nationalities derive particular value from their unmatched Settlement Freedom, thereby boosting the continent's Overall Value as well. Last year, geopolitical

and military tensions in the Eurasia region however caused a decrease in value for particularly Ukrainian nationality. Moreover, new restrictions on settlement by Russia resulted in reduced Settlement Freedom of the nationalities of Ukraine, Armenia, Azerbaijan, and Moldova. Overall, however, European nationalities remain firmly on top of the QNI General Ranking as well as the QNI Settlement Freedom Ranking. Within the EU region specifically, the older EU Member States largely maintain their quality as both Internal and External Value remain stable. The new Member States – particularly Bulgaria, Romania and Croatia – greatly benefitted from EU integration and will continue to improve in the coming years.

The nationalities of the US and Canada, on the other hand, benefit primarily from very strong Internal Value, in particular their Economic Strength. Both nationalities are in the second group of very high quality nationalities, together with for example Japan, Singapore and Korea: those which cannot compete with the superb Settlement Freedom of EU nationalities, but are outperforming basically all other statuses.

South American nationalities score slightly above average with a regional mean of 39.54% – a value that will however continue to increase in the coming years as economic and political integration of the continent deepens.[5] As nationals of the majority of South American countries now enjoy settlement access throughout the region, further economic integration and economic development in the coming years makes South America definitely one of the most interesting regions in terms of the quality of nationalities.

By contrast, Central America and the Caribbean fall short of the global mean with a regional mean of 32.86%. Nationalities of this region generally score lower on the majority of sub-elements, although intra-region differences are substantial. However, the general lack of significant Settlement Freedom based on the nationality itself, as opposed to other factors, such as additional certificates based on particular skills or higher education as applied in CARICOM, prevents even the top-ranked nationalities in this region from matching the European, North American and some of the East Asian nationalities.

The Asian and the Pacific region has a regional mean of 31.44%, which is quite far below the global mean. However, Asian nationalities occupy positions in the entire spectrum of the QNI, from the very high quality tier (for example Japan, New Zealand, and Singapore) to the low quality tier (Myanmar, Pakistan, and Afghanistan) of the QNI. The wide variety in quality among the Asian nationalities is caused by substantial differences in Internal Value and Travel Freedom. East and Southeast Asian nationalities generally score higher on the internal parameters than the nationalities of Eurasia and South Asia, while they also benefit from superior Travel Freedom. Japan and Singapore continue to be unmatched in Travel Freedom Diversity and Weight. In 2015, moreover, the Republic of Korea experienced a major increase in visa-free or visa on arrival tourist and business travel. Accordingly, its nationality jumped from 17th place in 2014 to 4th place in 2015 on the QNI Travel Freedom Ranking

---

5   See also the special contribution by Diego Acosta on South America, pp 147

The nationalities of Africa and the Middle East have an overall lower value in comparison with all other regions. North Africa and the Middle East scores a mean value of 26.51%. Their nationalities particularly suffer from regional destabilization in recent years, which has had severe detrimental consequences for Peace and Stability, but also (indirectly) Human Development and Economic Strength. In the past five years, the nationalities of particularly Libya, Bahrain and Oman experienced major blows in Internal Value, while last year the Syria saw an unsurprising free fall on the QNI General Ranking from 140th position in 2014 to 152nd position this year.

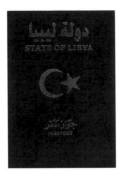  

Sub-Saharan nationalities have on average the least value with a regional mean of 24.27%. In addition to persistent instability, threats to peace, and a low level of both Human Development and Economic Strength, the Sub-Saharan Africa region also suffers from limited Settlement and Travel Freedom. The Economic Community of West African States (ECOWAS) provides for a more sophisticated form of economic integration, involving limited intra-organizational Settlement Freedom. Although the ECOWAS nationalities clearly outperform other Sub-Saharan nationalities, there is no advanced degree of integration comparable with, for example, the EU and MERCOSUR.

Trends in Settlement Freedom

Opportunities for foreign settlement diminished on average by 0.41%, mainly because Russia and Georgia restricted the full access opportunities for foreign nationals in 2014. Meanwhile, however, further political and economic integration in Europe and South America resulted in enhanced Settlement Freedom in those regions.

Until 2014, Russia granted *de facto* full access to the majority of the nationalities from Member States of the Commonwealth of Independent States (CIS), which in light of Russia's large economy and relatively high level of Human Development provided valuable opportunities for nationals of the CIS countries. When Russia restricted such access in 2014 except for nationals of Belarus and Kazakhstan, the Settlement Freedom of the other CIS nationalities suffered seriously. However, in 2015 Russia announced the liberalization of labor access for all

nationals of the Eurasian Economic Union – comprising Russia, Belarus, Kazakhstan, Armenia and Kyrgyzstan – so partial recovery of regional Settlement Freedom will be visible in the 2016 QNI.

In the 2000s, Georgia developed the most world's welcoming migration policy, allowing full access to nationals of 94 countries, in order to attract foreign investment and foster economic growth.[6] The country's decision to restrict full access in 2014 therefore negatively affected the global mean of Settlement Freedom. However, in May 2015 the Georgian government adopted legal amendments that re-introduced 360 day-long full access for foreign nationals. As Settlement Freedom is measured on 31 December of the preceding year,[7] Georgia's renewed liberal foreign settlement policy will again improve global Settlement Freedom in the 2016 QNI.

As a result of Russia and Georgia's combined restricted policies in 2015, the nationalities of the CIS Member States experienced the greatest fall in Settlement Freedom value compared with 2014.[8]

In Europe, the nationalities of Bulgaria, Romania and Croatia benefitted from further integration into the EU as a single working-living space and saw serious improvements in Settlement Freedom. On 1 January 2014, the final restrictions on the free movement of Bulgarian and Romanian workers were lifted. The effects of their subsequent full integration in the EU Internal Market are first visible in the 2015 QNI, and in that year both nationalities have experienced by far the largest increase in Settlement Freedom value.[9] After Croatia's accession to the EU on 1 July 2013, Croatian nationals already acquired full access to 14 EU Member States in 2013. Based on the cut-off date of 31 December 2013 for the measurement of Settlement Freedom in 2014 led to a massive increase in Settlement Freedom in the 2014 QNI. In 2014, Croatians also gained full access to two EEA countries – Norway and Iceland – which resulted in a further respectable improvement in Settlement Freedom in the 2015 QNI. Moreover, as nationals of Croatia have received additional labor access to other EU Member States in 2015, their nationality will continue to improve in the coming year.

6   See the special contribution by Laure Delcour on Georgia, pp 164

7   See Methodology, pp 9

8   See D. Settlement Freedom of Nationalities, Fallers in 2014–2015, pp 123

9   See D. Settlement Freedom of Nationalities, Risers in 2014–2015, pp 123

Regional integration in South America has boosted Settlement Freedom in the region.[10] Following the implementation of the MERCOSUR Residence Agreement in 2009, South American nationalities benefit from extensive free movement throughout the continent (not confined to the MERCOSUR Member States). Only Venezuela, Suriname and Guyana are, up to now, excluded from  this Settlement Freedom arrangement. Colombian nationality first benefitted from regional Settlement Freedom in 2013, which is visible in the sharp value increase between the 2013 QNI and the 2014 QNI. The most prominent riser in the 2015 QNI is however the nationality of Ecuador. As Ecuadorian nationals acquired Settlement Freedom in respect of Argentina, Bolivia, Brazil, Colombia, Paraguay, and Uruguay, the Ecuadoran nationality jumped from 91st to 67th position on the QNI General Ranking, and from 42th to 23th position on the QNI Settlement Freedom Ranking.[11]

Trends in Travel Freedom

Last year's most positive trend was a slight enhancement of global Travel Freedom. In comparison to the 2014 QNI, the global average of Travel Freedom value improved by 0.30%. Moldovan nationality saw the most serious improvement in Travel Freedom, as visa requirements for the Schengen area were lifted in 2014. This enabled Moldovan nationals to enjoy 26 addition visa-free or visa on arrival travel and business destinations. Other nationalities, including Mauritius and the Seychelles, experienced a respectable increase in the  number of destinations that could be visited visa-free or by visa on arrival for tourist and business purposes due to the opening up of visa-free tourist and business travel to the Schengen area for the holders of those nationalities.

In addition, after the general cut-off date of 1 May 2015, the EU decided to lift visa restrictions for multiple nationalities enabling visa-free travel to the Schengen area. From 7 May 2015, nationals of the United Arab Emirates have visa-free travel to the Schengen area for tourist and business stays up to 90 days. Georgian and Ukrainian nationals are expected to benefit from visa-free travel to the Schengen area by the end of 2016. These developments will boost the Travel Freedom of the nationalities of United Arab Emirates and possibly Georgia in the 2016 QNI. Ukrainian nationality will see a similar value increase in the 2017 QNI.

10   See also the special contribution on South America by Diego Acosta, pp 147

11   See B: The Quality of Nationalities, Risers in 2014–2015, pp 56

B – THE QUALITY OF NATIONALITIES

6 Nationalities of the world in 2015

The QNI General Ranking

	Nationality	Value 2015	Change in value 2014-2015	Change in value 2011-2015
1	Germany	83.1	0.0	+0.1
2	Denmark	83.0	+0.2	+1.7
3	Finland	82.0	-0.2	+0.5
4	Norway	81.7	+0.5	+0.2
5	Sweden	81.6	-0.1	+0.2
5	Iceland	81.6	+0.5	+1.1
6	Ireland	81.0	-0.2	+0.3
6	Austria	81.0	+0.3	+0.1
7	France	80.9	+0.1	-0.6
8	Switzerland	80.7	-0.3	0.0
9	Netherlands	80.3	-0.1	+0.4
10	Belgium	80.2	-0.2	-0.2
11	UK	80.1	-0.1	-0.8
12	Liechtenstein	80.0	-0.1	+0.2
13	Italy	79.8	-0.2	-0.4
13	Spain	79.8	0.0	+0.2
14	Luxembourg	79.3	-0.3	-0.8
15	Czech Republic	79.1	+1.0	+6.8
16	Portugal	78.9	+0.1	+0.1
17	Slovenia	78.8	+0.4	+4.2
18	Hungary	78.0	+0.7	+6.8
19	Slovakia	77.9	+1.1	+6.5
20	Estonia	76.7	+1.0	+7.0
20	Poland	76.7	+0.6	+5.0
21	Greece	76.5	-0.4	+1.2
22	Malta	76.4	-0.1	+2.8
23	Lithuania	76.2	+0.9	+6.2
24	Latvia	76.0	+0.7	+7.1
25	Cyprus	73.4	+0.4	+0.7
26	Romania	72.6	+9.8	+13.6
27	Bulgaria	72.4	+10.2	+14.2
	(European Union)	67.4	-0.6	-1.0
28	US	63.5	-0.9	-0.3

	Nationality	Value 2015	Change in value 2014-2015	Change in value 2011-2015
29	Croatia	58.3	+2.5	+17.5
30	Japan	56.2	-1.2	-1.2
31	New Zealand	53.4	-0.9	0.0
32	Canada	52.7	-0.9	+0.4
33	Australia	52.5	-0.7	-0.6
34	Chile	52.3	+2.4	+6.9
35	Singapore	51.9	-1.0	+0.2
36	Korea (Republic of)	50.8	0.0	+2.6
37	Argentina	50.4	+0.7	+2.3
38	Brazil	49.1	-0.3	+1.9
39	San Marino	48.5	-0.8	+0.1
40	Monaco	48.4	-0.6	-1.0
41	Uruguay	47.7	-0.2	+2.0
42	Andorra	47.0	-1.1	-0.3
43	Brunei Darussalam	46.5	-1.0	-0.6
44	Malaysia	46.3	-0.8	-0.4
45	Hong Kong. China (SAR)	44.4	-0.2	+0.3
46	Taiwan	44.0	0.0	+13.1
47	Paraguay	42.7	+0.2	+1.4
48	Bahamas	42.5	+0.6	+1.5
49	Israel	41.9	-0.7	-0.2
50	Mauritius	40.6	+0.4	+1.9
51	Barbados	39.8	-1.5	-1.0
52	Macao	39.5	0.4	2.2
53	Mexico	39.4	-1.0	-0.8
54	Costa Rica	39.1	-0.4	-1.0
55	Venezuela	39.0	0.0	+0.7
56	Seychelles	38.3	+0.6	+6.1
57	Panama	38.1	-0.6	+1.4
58	Antigua and Barbuda	38.0	-1.4	-0.7
59	St. Kitts and Nevis	37.7	-1.5	-0.3
60	China	37.4	+0.8	+4.1
60	Russian Federation	37.4	+0.6	+3.3
60	Qatar	37.4	-0.3	-0.7
61	Peru	36.5	+0.4	+2.0
62	United Arab Emirates	36.3	-0.2	+0.2
63	Kuwait	36.0	-0.8	-0.8
64	Serbia	35.8	-0.2	+1.8
65	Montenegro	34.6	-0.6	+0.4

	Nationality	Value 2015	Change in value 2014-2015	Change in value 2011-2015
66	Macedonia	34.4	+0.1	+1.3
67	Ecuador	34.3	+5.1	+6.5
68	El Salvador	34.0	-1.5	-1.1
68	Saudi Arabia	34.0	-0.6	+0.9
69	Guatemala	33.9	-1.0	-0.6
70	Turkey	33.8	+0.8	+1.5
71	Bolivia	33.7	+0.4	+2.4
72	Honduras	33.6	-0.6	0.0
73	Oman	33.4	-0.5	-2.0
74	Bosnia and Herzegovina	33.3	+0.1	+6.5
75	Bahrain	33.2	-1.2	-2.1
76	Nicaragua	33.1	+0.1	+0.5
77	Cape Verde	32.7	0.0	+1.2
77	Moldova	32.7	+4.1	+4.6
78	Trinidad and Tobago	32.6	-0.7	-0.3
79	Ghana	32.3	+0.4	-0.1
80	Albania	32.0	-0.3	+6.3
81	Colombia	31.7	+0.2	+6.6
82	Belarus	31.6	-0.6	+0.6
83	Kazakhstan	31.1	+0.5	+2.9
84	Gambia	30.7	+0.3	-0.4
85	Benin	30.4	+0.5	+0.9
86	St. Lucia	30.3	-1.4	-0.6
87	Ukraine	30.2	-2.2	+0.2
88	Senegal	30.1	+0.4	+1.0
89	South Africa	30.0	-0.2	-0.2
90	St. Vincent and the Grenadines	29.9	-1.6	-0.9
91	Grenada	29.8	-0.5	0.0
92	Sierra Leone	29.5	+0.4	-4.3
93	Dominica	29.3	-1.4	+3.6
93	Togo	29.3	+0.1	+0.6
94	Suriname	28.8	-0.3	+1.2
95	Belize	28.7	-0.9	-1.3
96	Maldives	28.5	+0.1	+1.3
97	Côte d'Ivoire	28.4	+0.7	+0.5
98	Guyana	28.3	+0.1	+2.2
99	Burkina Faso	28.2	+0.5	+0.4
100	Jamaica	28.1	+0.2	-0.1
101	Thailand	28.0	-1.0	+0.7

	Nationality	Value 2015	Change in value 2014-2015	Change in value 2011-2015
101	Nigeria	28.0	+0.1	-0.4
102	India	27.9	+0.1	+1.4
103	Georgia	27.8	+0.9	+2.3
103	Liberia	27.8	+0.6	+1.1
103	Mali	27.8	0.0	+0.3
104	Botswana	27.6	-1.1	-1.2
104	Guinea	27.6	+0.1	+0.1
105	Indonesia	27.4	0.3	+1.9
106	Cuba	27.3	-1.1	+0.1
107	Azerbaijan	27.1	-1.4	-0.1
108	Tunisia	26.9	+0.1	-1.2
108	Niger	26.9	+0.3	+1.0
109	Guinea-Bissau	26.2	0.0	-0.1
109	(Non-citizen) Latvia	26.2	0.0	+0.4
109	Namibia	26.2	+0.2	+0.4
110	Armenia	26.1	-1.7	-0.7
111	Uzbekistan	25.4	-1.5	-0.9
112	Philippines	25.2	+0.2	+1.5
113	Mongolia	25.0	+0.5	+1.9
114	Dominican Republic	24.8	-0.8	-3.6
115	Bhutan	24.7	+0.3	+2.3
116	Tajikistan	24.6	-1.0	-1.2
117	Zambia	24.4	+0.1	+0.7
118	Jordan	24.3	0.0	+0.4
118	Lesotho	24.3	+0.4	+0.7
119	Papua New Guinea	24.1	+0.3	+0.8
119	Kyrgyzstan	24.1	-1.7	-1.5
120	Vietnam	24.0	+0.3	+1.1
121	Morocco	23.8	+0.4	+0.1
121	Kosovo	23.8	+0.2	+1.4
122	Swaziland	23.7	+0.3	-0.2
123	Turkmenistan	23.4	-0.4	+0.3
124	Algeria	23.3	-0.2	-0.2
125	Gabon	23.0	0.0	+0.7
126	Laos	22.9	+0.2	+1.1
126	Timor-Leste	22.9	-0.1	+0.8
127	Iran	22.8	-0.2	+0.4
128	Kenya	22.7	+0.3	+0.6
129	Egypt	22.6	-0.6	-1.2

	Nationality	Value 2015	Change in value 2014-2015	Change in value 2011-2015
129	Tanzania	22.6	-0.2	+0.3
129	Sri Lanka	22.6	+0.2	+0.5
130	Libya	22.5	0.0	-2.4
131	Cambodia	22.0	+0.3	+2.0
131	Lebanon	22.0	-1.0	-0.1
132	Malawi	21.9	+0.1	+0.2
133	Sao Tome and Principe	21.6	0.0	+0.7
134	Uganda	21.5	+0.1	+0.6
135	Nepal	20.9	0.0	0.0
136	Zimbabwe	20.7	+0.1	+0.7
137	Madagascar	20.5	+0.3	+0.6
138	Bangladesh	20.2	+0.2	+0.1
139	Mauritania	20.1	-0.4	+0.3
140	Equatorial Guinea	20.0	-0.2	0.0
140	Haiti	20.0	+0.1	+1.1
141	Palestinian Territory	19.9	-0.2	+0.6
142	Congo	19.8	-0.4	-0.4
143	Myanmar	19.7	+0.3	+1.8
144	Comoros	19.5	0.0	+0.5
145	Angola	19.4	0.0	+0.7
146	Cameroon	19.3	-0.1	+0.4
147	Djibouti	19.1	-0.1	-0.4
148	Rwanda	18.9	+0.1	+0.7
149	Mozambique	18.8	-0.1	0.0
150	Yemen	18.4	0.0	+0.6
151	Iraq	18.0	-1.2	-0.2
152	Syria	17.3	-2.1	-4.2
153	Pakistan	17.1	-0.1	-0.6
154	Ethiopia	17.0	-0.2	+1.0
155	Chad	16.8	-0.2	+1.4
156	Burundi	16.7	+0.3	+0.9
157	Sudan	16.1	-0.3	+1.0
158	Eritrea	15.9	-0.2	+0.3
159	Central African Republic	15.3	-0.7	-1.7
160	Afghanistan	14.4	-0.1	+0.2
161	Congo (Democratic Republic of the)	14.3	-0.3	+0.3

General statistics

In 2015
- The global mean of the Quality of Nationalities was 38.70
- The global median was 30.90

In 2014–2015
- The Quality of Nationalities on average improved by 0.02 points
- 88 nationalities lost value
- 81 nationalities gained value
- 16 nationalities remained stable in value

In 2011–2015
- The Quality of Nationalities on average improved by 1.12 points
- 53 nationalities lost value
- 125 nationalities gained value
- Seven nationalities remained stable in value

Germany

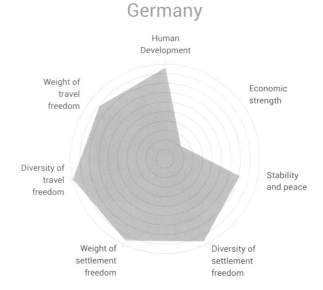

Congo (Democratic Republic of the)

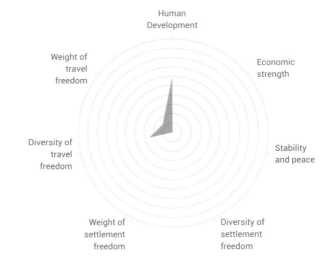

Risers and fallers in 2014–2015

Top 5 risers

	Nationality	Change in value	Change in ranking
1	Bulgaria	+10.2	+2
2	Romania	+9.8	+2
3	Ecuador	+5.1	+24
4	Moldova	+4.1	+18
5	Croatia	+2.5	+2

The Bulgarian nationality experienced a substantial increase in external value last year. Apart from a slight increase in Stability and Peace, internal quality remained roughly stable. The further removal of restrictions on free movement of Bulgarian passport holders within the EU resulted in all round external quality improvement. Visa restrictions for Bulgarian passport holders were lifted by eight destinations, resulting in a significant improvement of both Diversity and Weight of Travel Freedom. Its Settlement Freedom likewise benefitted from an increase of eight additional settlement destinations, including large EU Member States such as the UK and Spain. Bulgaria's ranking moved 'only' two places upward as a result of the relatively high quality of EU nationalities.

Trends for Romanian nationality are almost identical to those for Bulgaria. Stability and Peace demonstrated a slight improvement. Settlement Freedom values also increased substantially after the opening up of eight EU Member States' markets for Romanian nationals. Visa restrictions were lifted by seven destinations, resulting in an overall value increase just below that of Bulgaria.

The nationality of Ecuador made a gigantic leap of 24 ranks forward in the QNI General Ranking. This steep rise particularly has to do with a serious extension of free movement, residence and working rights for Ecuadorians in the region. In 2015, Ecuadorian nationals received full access to Argentina, Bolivia, Brazil, Colombia, Paraguay and Uruguay due to the implementation of the MERCOSUR Residence agreement in Ecuador.[12] This means its Weight of Settlement Freedom was more than six times more valuable in comparison to 2014. Moreover, the number of destinations giving Ecuadorian nationals visa-free or visa on arrival access to their territory increased by four, although this had less impact on overall quality than the vast improvement in Settlement Freedom.

Nationals of the Republic of Moldova benefitted primarily from a significant decrease in visa restrictions. Travel Freedom Diversity rose from 59 destinations in 2014 to 89 destinations in 2015 after the introduction of visa-free travel to the Schengen area in 2014. Consequently, Moldovan nationality experienced a 50% increase in Travel Freedom Diversity value, and even a 90% increase in the value of Travel Freedom Weight. Moldova's Settlement Freedom also improved, doubling Diversity from two to four free settlement destinations.

Croatian passport holders, like many nationalities, experienced little increase in internal value. Their Settlement Freedom Diversity and Weight improved slightly with one additional destination (Iceland). Visa restrictions were lifted by nine destinations, giving Croatian nationals visa-free or visa on arrival access to 138 destinations compared with 129 in 2014.

12   Acuerdo Ministerial No. 000031 (2 April 2014)

Top 5 fallers

	Nationality	Change in value	Change in ranking
1	Ukraine	-2.2	-8
2	Syria	-2.1	-12
3	Armenia	-1.7	-11
4	Kyrgyzstan	-1.7	-11
5	St. Vincent and the Grenadines	-1.6	-8

The nationality of Ukraine lost value on multiple elements as a result of recent economic and political instability. Its Economic Strength decreased mildly, but Stability and Peace deteriorated substantially, leading to a weakening of the corresponding value by 11%. The Diversity of Settlement Freedom halved from four settlement destinations in 2014 to two in 2015 with Russia and Georgia closing access. While the Diversity of Travel Freedom increased from 77 to 79 destinations, Weight of Travel Freedom did not benefit from this and actually deteriorated slightly.

The free fall of Syrian nationality hardly needs explanation. All elements were subject to decreasing value. Human Development, and Stability and Peace indicators worsened directly as a result of the ongoing civil war. Passport holders of the Syria did not enjoy any Freedom of Settlement in 2014 or in 2015. Travel Freedom also decreased substantially from 39 visa-free or visa on arrival destinations in 2014 to 33 one year later. That the overall decrease in value and the loss of 12 ranks seems somewhat limited in the context of the disastrous situation in which the country finds itself, is solely caused by the fact that the Syrian nationality's value was already extremely low.

Armenian nationality experienced a very small improvement in internal value, caused by a minor increase in Stability and Peace. Visa restrictions for nationals remained stable, however passport holders' Settlement Freedom Diversity decreased from three destinations (Georgia, Kyrgyzstan and Russia) to one – only Kyrgyzstan remaining. Particularly, closed settlement access to Russia detrimentally affected the Armenian nationality's Settlement Freedom Weight.

Nationals of Kyrgyzstan were confronted with reduced Settlement Freedom, from having full access to Russia, Georgia, and Armenia in 2014, to only having such access to Armenia one year later. Both Settlement Freedom Diversity and Settlement Freedom Weight decreased by twice their value. Kyrgyzstan passport holders did gain access to two more visa-free or visa on arrival travel destinations, Travel Freedom Diversity rising from 56 to 58. However, this hardly affected the nationality's overall value and could not compensate the substantial loss in Settlement Freedom.

The nationality of St. Vincent and the Grenadines only provided free settlement access to Georgia, but this access was closed in 2015. The Travel Freedom of passport holders remained stable with 92 visa-free or visa on arrival destinations. The decrease in value is further attributed to Stability and Peace, which lost approximately 8% of its value.

Uzbekistan nationality gave access to an additional two travel destinations with visa-free or visa on arrival (52 in 2014 and 54 in 2015). However, the country experienced a decrease in Stability and Peace, and Diversity and Weight of Settlement Freedom. Both lost half of their value, as a result of closing free settlement access to Russia and Georgia.

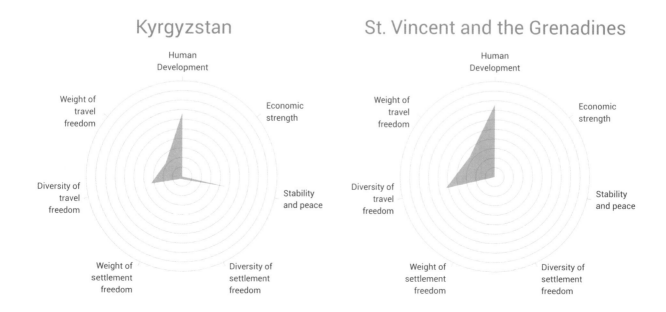

Risers and fallers in 2011–2015

Top 5 risers

	Nationality	Change in value	Change in ranking
1	Croatia	+17.5	+19
2	Bulgaria	+14.3	+1
3	Romania	+13.6	+1
4	Taiwan	+13.1	+31
5	Latvia	+7.1	+1

Croatian nationality benefitted from the greatest increase in value as a result of its accession to the EU in 2013. Its internal value improved slightly, but the overwhelming part of its rise is attributed to Settlement Freedom and Travel Freedom. In 2011, nationals had no free settlement access to any other country. In 2015, Settlement Freedom Diversity had grown to 16 possible destinations. Croatian nationality also benefitted from a substantial increase in Travel Freedom Diversity, from 116 visa-free or visa on arrival destinations in 2011 to 138 in 2015.

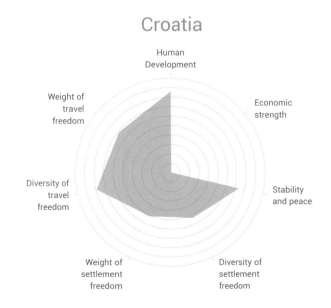

Croatia

Bulgarian nationality experienced further integration in the EU internal market. In 2011 restrictions on the Settlement Freedom of Bulgarians still existed in some EU Member States, and Bulgarian passport holders could settle freely in 17 countries. Five years later, these restrictions have been fully removed, bringing Settlement Freedom Diversity to 29 countries. Simultaneously, Travel Freedom Diversity was increased from 133 travel destinations in 2011 to 149 in 2015.

Nationals of Romania saw a similar value increase as the Bulgarians. Settlement Freedom increased from 17 full access destinations to 29 after the final obstructions to free movement of Romanians had been removed. In addition, the Travel Freedom Diversity rose from 136 to 148 destinations.

The nationality of Taiwan experienced an increase that was almost entirely attributable to hugely improved Travel Freedom. In addition to a very small increase in Stability and Peace, Taiwan's Travel Freedom Diversity rose from 60 visa-free or visa on arrival destinations in 2011 to 132 destinations in 2015. This more than doubled the nationality of Taiwan's Travel Freedom Diversity score, and almost tripled its Travel Freedom Weight. In particular the abolishment of visa requirements for access to the Schengen area contributed to this effect. As China announced the lifting of visa restrictions in 2015, after the cut-off date of 1 May 2015, the value of Taiwanese nationality is likely to improve further in 2016.

The nationality of Latvia suffered from a minor deterioration in Stability and Peace over the last five years. However, this loss was overcompensated by the removal of the final restrictions to Latvian's Settlement Freedom within the EU: from 26 full access destinations in 2011, Latvian nationals could settle freely in 29 destinations in 2015. Moreover, Latvia benefitted from a substantial increase in Travel Freedom Diversity. Visa-free or visa on arrival travel existed to 139 travel destinations in 2011, a number that grew to 158 in 2015. However, it must be stressed that Latvia has two nationalities for the purposes of QNI: the 'ordinary' Latvian nationality and the Latvian status for non-citizens.[13] The serious quality improvement applies only to the 'ordinary' nationality of Latvia and not to the status of non-citizens, which does not grant any right to free movement within the EU. As a result of the quality increase, the divergence between 'ordinary' Latvian nationality and the Latvian status for non-citizens continues to increase.

13   See further pp 12

Top 5 fallers

	Nationality	Change in value	Change in ranking
1	Sierra Leone	-4.3	-26
2	Dominican Republic	-3.6	-29
3	Libya	-2.4	-22
4	Bahrain	-2.1	-15
5	Oman	-2.0	-13

The nationality of Sierra Leone lost significant value on both internal and external elements. Although there has been a slight increase in Human Development, Stability and Peace deteriorated over the past five years. Settlement Freedom Diversity remained stable at 12 full access countries, which are all Member States of ECOWAS. However, the loss of substantial value and 27 ranks is mainly caused by tightened visa restrictions. Travel Freedom Diversity comprised 113 visa-free or visa on arrival destinations in 2011. Five years later this number has almost been halved to 65 destinations.

The nationality of the Dominican Republic has lost the most positions over the past five years after a freefall of 30 ranks. Its internal value has remained fairly stable, however, Settlement Freedom was reduced to zero destinations, and Travel Freedom Diversity suffered substantial harm, as visa-free or visa on arrival travel was limited to 53 destinations in 2015, compared with 80 such destinations in 2011.

Libyan nationality unsurprisingly lost substantial value in many aspects. Internal value diminished as a result of the ongoing civil war, which deteriorated Stability and Peace but also detrimentally affected Human Development. Settlement Freedom was and continues to be non-existent. In addition, passport holders are faced with a marginal loss in Travel Freedom Diversity, which decreased from 39 visa-free or visa on arrival destinations in 2011 to 38 in 2015.

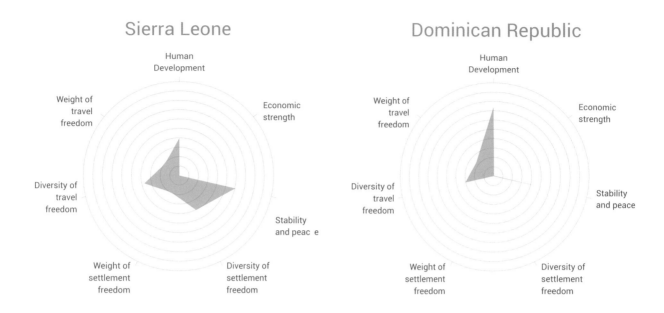

Nationals of Bahrain were confronted with threats to Stability and Peace, reducing the value of this element with almost 19%. Free settlement in Georgia was repealed, although Bahrain nationality still maintains a Settlement Freedom Diversity value of five due to free settlement in the other countries of the Gulf Cooperation Council.

The nationality of Oman experienced trends similar to that of Bahrain. Its nationality benefitted from a slight improvement in Travel Freedom Diversity, which increased from 61 visa-free or visa on arrival destinations in 2011 to 66 such destinations in 2015. However, the main source of quality loss was a substantial reduction in Stability and Peace, the value of which decreased by almost 22%.

Very high development nationalities

	Nationality	Value 2015	Change in value 2014-2015	Change in value 2011-2015	Overall ranking 2015
1	Germany	83.1	0.0	+0.1	1
2	Denmark	83.0	+0.2	+1.7	2
3	Finland	82.0	-0.2	+0.5	3
4	Norway	81.7	+0.5	+0.2	4
5	Iceland	81.6	+0.5	+1.1	5
5	Sweden	81.6	-0.2	+0.2	5
6	Austria	81.0	+0.3	+0.2	6
6	Ireland	81.0	-0.2	+0.4	6
7	France	80.9	+0.1	-0.6	7
8	Switzerland	80.7	-0.3	0.0	8
9	Netherlands	80.3	-0.1	+0.4	9
10	Belgium	80.2	-0.2	-0.2	10
11	UK	80.1	-0.1	-0.8	11
12	Liechtenstein	80.0	-0.1	+0.2	12
13	Spain	79.8	0.0	+0.3	13
13	Italy	79.8	-0.2	-0.4	13
14	Luxembourg	79.3	-0.3	-0.7	14
15	Czech Republic	79.1	+1.0	+6.8	15
16	Portugal	78.9	+0.1	+0.1	16
17	Slovenia	78.8	+0.4	4.2	17
18	Hungary	78.0	0.7	6.8	18
19	Slovakia	77.9	1,1	+6.5	19
20	Estonia	76.7	+0.9	+7.0	20
20	Poland	76.7	+0.6	5.0	20
21	Greece	76.5	-0.4	+1.2	21
22	Malta	76.4	-0.1	+2.8	22
23	Lithuania	76.2	0.9	6.2	23
24	Latvia	76.0	0.7	7.1	24
25	Cyprus	73.4	+0.4	+0.6	25
26	US	63.5	-0.9	-0.3	28
27	Croatia	58.3	+2.5	+17.5	29
28	Japan	56.2	-1.2	-1.2	30
29	New Zealand	53.4	-0.9	0.0	31
30	Canada	52.7	-0.9	+0.4	32
31	Australia	52.5	-0.7	-0.6	33
32	Chile	52.3	+2.4	+6.9	34
33	Singapore	51.9	-1.0	+0.2	35

	Nationality	Value 2015	Change in value 2014-2015	Change in value 2011-2015	Overall ranking 2015
34	Korea (Republic of)	50.8	0.0	+2.6	36
35	Argentina	50.4	+0.7	+2.3	37
36	San Marino	48.5	-0.8	+0.1	39
37	Monaco	48.4	-0.6	-1.0	40
38	Andorra	47.0	-1.1	-0.3	42
39	Brunei Darussalam	46.5	-1.0	-0.6	43
40	Hong Kong. China (SAR)	44.4	-0.2	+0.3	45
41	Taiwan	44.0	0.0	+13.1	46
42	Israel	41.9	-0.7	-0.2	49
43	Qatar	37.4	-0.3	-0.7	60
44	United Arab Emirates	36.3	-0.2	+0.2	62
45	Kuwait	36.0	-0.8	-0.8	63
46	Montenegro	34.6	-0.6	+0.4	65
47	Saudi Arabia	34.0	-0.6	+0.9	68
48	Bahrain	33.2	-1.2	-2.1	75

Mean: 64.35
Median: 76.20

Very high development nationalities are those that are associated with a HDI score of more than 0.800. The majority of very high development nationalities are also in the very high quality tier of the QNI. However, there is a clear divergence in value between the nationalities of the EU, which excel due to their superb External Value, and the other nationalities in this category. Very high development nationalities in Middle East and Asia are associated with less Travel Freedom and, particularly, far less Settlement Freedom.

Over the past five years, the most notable movements are the quality increase of Middle and Eastern European nationalities, which have acquired further settlement access in the rest of the EU. Outside of the EU, the nationality of Taiwan saw a vast increase in quality, after its Diversity of Travel Freedom improved from 60 visa-free or visa on arrival destinations in 2011 to 132 such destinations in 2015.

High development nationalities

	Nationality	Value 2015	Change in value 2014-2015	Change in value 2011-2015	Overall ranking 2015
1	Romania	72.6	+9.8	+13.6	26
2	Bulgaria	72.4	+10.2	+14.2	27
3	Brazil	49.1	-0.3	+1.9	38
4	Uruguay	47.7	-0.2	+2.0	41
5	Malaysia	46.3	-0.8	-0.4	44
6	Bahamas	42.5	+0.6	+1.5	48
7	Mauritius	40.6	+0.4	+1.9	50
8	Barbados	39.8	-1.5	-1	51
9	Macao	39.5	+0.4	+2.2	52
10	Mexico	39.4	-1.0	-0.8	53
11	Costa Rica	39.1	-0.4	-1.0	54
12	Venezuela	39.0	0.0	+0.7	55
13	Seychelles	38.3	+0.6	+6.1	56
14	Panama	38.1	-0.6	+1.4	57
15	Antigua and Barbuda	38.0	-1.4	-0.7	58
16	St. Kitts and Nevis	37.7	-1.5	-0.3	59
17	China	37.4	+0.8	+4.1	60
17	Russian Federation	37.4	+0.6	+3.3	60
18	Peru	36.5	+0.4	+2.0	61
19	Serbia	35.8	-0.2	+1.8	64
20	Macedonia	34.4	+0.1	+1.3	66
21	Ecuador	34.3	+5.1	+6.5	67
22	Turkey	33.8	+0.8	+1.5	70
23	Oman	33.4	-0.5	-2.0	73
24	Bosnia and Herzegovina	33.3	+0.1	+6.5	74
25	Trinidad and Tobago	32.6	-0.7	-0.3	78
26	Albania	32.0	-0.3	+6.3	80
27	Colombia	31.7	+0.2	+6.6	81
28	Belarus	31.6	-0.6	+0.6	82
29	Kazakhstan	31.1	+0.5	+2.9	83
30	St. Lucia	30.3	-1.4	-0.6	86
31	Ukraine	30.2	-2.2	+0.2	87
32	St. Vincent and the Grenadines	29.9	-1.6	-0.9	90
33	Grenada	29.8	-0.5	0.0	91
34	Dominica	29.3	-1.4	+3.6	93
35	Suriname	28.8	-0.3	+1.2	94
36	Belize	28.7	-0.9	-1.3	95

	Nationality	Value 2015	Change in value 2014-2015	Change in value 2011-2015	Overall ranking 2015
37	Maldives	28.5	+0.1	+1.3	96
38	Jamaica	28.1	+0.2	-0.1	100
39	Thailand	28.0	-1.0	+0.7	101
40	Georgia	27.8	+0.9	+2.3	103
41	Cuba	27.3	-1.1	+0.1	106
42	Azerbaijan	27.1	-1.4	-0.1	107
43	Tunisia	26.9	+0.1	-1.2	108
44	Armenia	26.1	-1.7	-0.7	110
45	Mongolia	25.0	+0.5	+1.9	113
46	Dominican Republic	24.8	-0.8	-3.6	114
47	Jordan	24.3	0.0	+0.4	118
48	Kosovo	23.8	+0.2	+1.4	121
49	Algeria	23.3	-0.2	-0.2	124
50	Iran	22.8	-0.2	+0.4	127
51	Sri Lanka	22.6	+0.2	+0.5	129
52	Libya	22.5	0.0	-2.4	130
53	Lebanon	22.0	-1.0	-0.1	131

Mean: 33.95
Median: 31.85

High development nationalities are those that are associated with a HDI of between 0.700 and 0.799. With the exception of Bulgaria and Romania, the high development nationalities are in the high and medium quality tier of the QNI. Indeed, many highly developed countries have unattractive nationalities. This is in some cases partially caused by a low score on Stability and Peace, but often persistent conflict and instability will negatively affect Human Development as well.

The lower quality of nationalities of the bottom High Development nationalities is therefore primarily caused by low external value. Many of the abovementioned passports indeed provide no or very limited Settlement Freedom Diversity. Moreover, Travel Freedom Diversity and Weight is limited for many highly developed nationalities, in particular those in the Russia and Eurasia regions.

As a result, the High Development nationalities have a mean of 33.95 and a median of 31.85. This is significantly lower than the global mean (38.70) and only slightly higher than the global median (30.90). Moreover, it is far below the average values of, for example, the G20 and OECD nationalities. High quality nationalities are therefore not primarily associated with high HDI scores. Instead, they are specifically concentrated in the industrialized regions, which provide external values far exceeding the global average.

Medium development nationalities

	Nationality	Value 2015	Change in value 2014-2015	Change in value 2011-2015	Overall ranking 2015
1	Paraguay	42.7	+0.2	+1.4	47
2	El Salvador	34.0	-1.5	-1.1	68
3	Guatemala	33.9	-1.0	-0.6	69
4	Bolivia	33.7	+0.4	+2.4	71
5	Honduras	33.6	-0.6	0.0	72
6	Nicaragua	33.1	+0.1	+0.5	76
7	Cape Verde	32.7	0.0	+1.2	77
7	Moldova	32.7	+4.1	+4.6	77
8	Ghana	32.3	+0.4	-0.1	79
9	South Africa	30.0	-0.2	-0.2	89
10	Guyana	28.3	+0.1	+2.2	98
11	India	27.9	+0.1	+1.4	102
12	Botswana	27.6	-1.1	-1.2	104
13	Indonesia	27.4	+0.3	+1.9	105
14	Namibia	26.2	+0.2	+0.4	109
15	Uzbekistan	25.4	-1.5	-0.9	111
16	Philippines	25.2	+0.2	+1.5	112
17	Bhutan	24.7	+0.3	+2.3	115
18	Tajikistan	24.6	-1.0	-1.2	116
19	Zambia	24.4	+0.1	+0.7	117
20	Kyrgyzstan	24.1	-1.7	-1.5	119
21	Viet Nam	24.0	+0.3	+1.1	120
22	Morocco	23.8	+0.4	+0.1	121
23	Turkmenistan	23.4	-0.4	+0.3	123
24	Gabon	23.0	0.0	+0.7	125
25	Laos	22.9	+0.2	+1.1	126
25	Timor-Leste	22.9	-0.1	+0.8	126
26	Egypt	22.6	-0.6	-1.2	129
27	Cambodia	22.0	+0.3	+2.0	131
28	Sao Tome and Principe	21.6	0.0	+0.7	133
29	Bangladesh	20.2	+0.2	+0.1	138
30	Equatorial Guinea	20.0	-0.2	0.0	140
31	Palestinian Territory	19.9	-0.2	+0.6	141
32	Congo	19.8	-0.4	-0.4	142
33	Iraq	18.0	-1.2	-0.2	151
34	Syria	17.3	-2.1	-4.2	152

Mean: 26.28

Median: 24.65

Medium development nationalities are those that are associated with a HDI between 0.550 and 0.700. These nationalities have a medium to low quality. None of the medium development nationalities scores very high on the QNI General Ranking, because their external value generally falls short of that of the high development nationalities. However, the spread of medium development nationalities in the QNI General Ranking is substantial, from 47th (Paraguay) to 152rd (Syria).

Consequently, the quality of medium development nationalities overlaps to a significant extent with that of low development nationalities. This is primarily caused by the comparatively high overall value of the ECOWAS nationalities.[14] Overall, the mean of medium development nationalities is 26.28, substantially below the global mean (38.70). The same applies to their median value (24.65, global median 30.90).

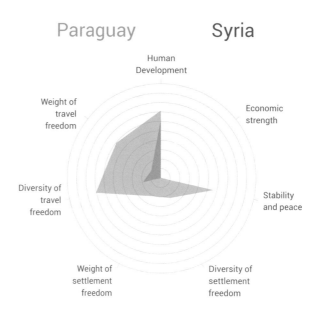

Paraguay   Syria

Low development nationalities

	Nationality	Value 2015	Change in value 2014-2015	Change in value 2011-2015	Overall ranking 2015
1	Gambia	30.7	+0.3	-0.4	84
2	Benin	30.4	+0.5	+0.9	85
3	Senegal	30.1	+0.4	+1.0	88
4	Sierra Leone	29.5	+0.4	-4.3	92
5	Togo	29.3	+0.1	+0.6	93
6	Côte d'Ivoire	28.4	+0.7	+0.5	97
7	Burkina Faso	28.2	+0.5	+0.4	99
8	Nigeria	28.0	+0.1	-0.4	101
9	Liberia	27.8	+0.6	+1.1	103
9	Mali	27.8	0.0	+0.3	103
10	Guinea	27.6	+0.1	+0.1	104
11	Niger	26.9	+0.3	+1.0	108
12	Guinea-Bissau	26.2	0.0	-0.1	109
13	Lesotho	24.3	+0.4	+0.7	118
14	Papua New Guinea	24.1	+0.3	+0.8	119
15	Swaziland	23.7	+0.3	-0.2	122
16	Kenya	22.7	+0.3	+0.6	128
17	Tanzania	22.6	-0.2	+0.3	129
18	Malawi	21.9	+0.1	+0.2	132
19	Uganda	21.5	+0.1	+0.6	134
20	Nepal	20.9	0.0	0.0	135
21	Zimbabwe	20.7	+0.1	+0.7	136
22	Madagascar	20.5	+0.3	+0.6	137
23	Mauritania	20.1	-0.4	+0.3	139
24	Haiti	20.0	+0.1	+1.1	140
25	Myanmar	19.7	+0.3	+1.8	143
26	Comoros	19.5	0.0	+0.5	144
27	Angola	19.4	0.0	+0.7	145
28	Cameroon	19.3	-0.1	+0.4	146
29	Djibouti	19.1	-0.1	-0.4	147
30	Rwanda	18.9	+0.1	+0.7	148
31	Mozambique	18.8	-0.1	0.0	149
32	Yemen	18.4	0.0	+0.6	150
33	Pakistan	17.1	-0.1	-0.6	153
34	Ethiopia	17.0	-0.2	+1.0	154
35	Chad	16.8	-0.2	+1.4	155
36	Burundi	16.7	+0.3	+0.9	156

	Nationality	Value 2015	Change in value 2014-2015	Change in value 2011-2015	Overall ranking 2015
37	Sudan	16.1	-0.3	+1.0	157
38	Eritrea	15.9	-0.2	+0.3	158
39	Central African Republic	15.3	-0.7	-1.7	159
40	Afghanistan	14.4	-0.1	+0.2	160
41	Congo (Democratic Republic of the)	14.3	-0.3	+0.3	161

Mean: 22.16
Median: 20.80

Low development nationalities are those associated with a HDI below 0.550. These nationalities invariably are in the lower spectrum of the QNI General Ranking. Low development countries generally have lower scores on Economic Strength and Stability and Peace. In addition, their external value of nationality is mostly marginal. Nonetheless, values overlap significantly with the medium development nationalities. Overall, the low development nationalities have a mean value of 22.16 (global mean: 38.70) and a median of 20.80 (global median: 30.90).

Among the low development nationalities, the countries of ECOWAS clearly stand out. In spite of their low HDI, these nationalities are able to compensate with a substantial levels of Settlement Freedom Diversity and Weight, since nationals of one member are generally allowed to live and work freely in other members.

Gambia
Congo (Democratic Republic of the)

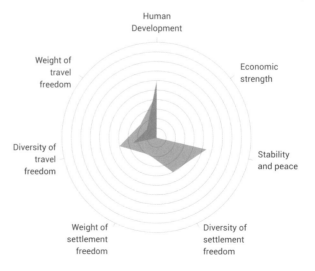

Nationalities of the G20

	Nationality	Value 2015	Change in value 2014-2015	Change in value 2011-2015	Overall ranking 2015
1	Germany	83.1	0.0	+0.1	1
2	France	80.9	+0.1	-0.6	7
3	UK	80.1	-0.1	-0.8	11
4	Italy	79.8	-0.2	-0.4	13
5	European Union	67.5	-0.6	-1.0	n/a
6	US	63.5	-0.9	-0.3	28
7	Japan	56.2	-1.2	-1.2	30
8	Canada	52.7	-0.9	+0.4	32
9	Australia	52.5	-0.7	-0.6	33
10	Korea (Republic of)	50.8	0.0	+2.6	36
11	Argentina	50.4	+0.7	+2.3	37
12	Brazil	49.1	-0.3	+1.9	38
13	Mexico	39.4	-1.0	-0.8	53
14	China	37.4	+0.8	+4.1	60
14	Russian Federation	37.4	+0.6	+3.3	60
15	Saudi Arabia	34.0	-0.6	+0.9	68
16	Turkey	33.8	+0.8	+1.5	70
17	South Africa	30.0	-0.2	-0.2	89
18	India	27.9	+0.1	+1.4	102
19	Indonesia	27.4	+0.3	+1.9	105

Mean: 52.21
Median: 50.60

The G20 consists of the 20 most important economies in the world. Founded in 1999, the organization provides a platform for high-level discussion on international financial stability and, more broadly, the state and development of the global economy. Its members – 19 individual countries and the EU – account for around 85% of world GDP and two-thirds of the world population.

The quality of G20 nationalities varies tremendously, from top 10 nationalities such as Germany and France, to medium to low scoring nationalities like India and Indonesia. On average however, G20 nationalities substantially outperform the world average with a mean of 52.21 (world mean: 38.70) and a median of 50.60 (world median: 30.90). This is attributed mainly to the high-performing nationalities, in particular those of the EU Member States which are also members of the G20. Nevertheless, globally influential G20 members including China, the Russian Federation and Saudi Arabia demonstrate that economic strength and political power are not sufficient reasons for high-quality nationalities. Their nationalities' weaknesses lie mainly in the field of external value: limited Settlement and Travel Freedom. Particularly the Weight of Travel Freedom suffers from visa restrictions to valuable first-world destinations.

Over the past five years, the quality of most G20 nationalities maintained or increased its value. China, the Russian Federation, the Republic of Korea and Argentina experienced substantial improvement of more than two points.

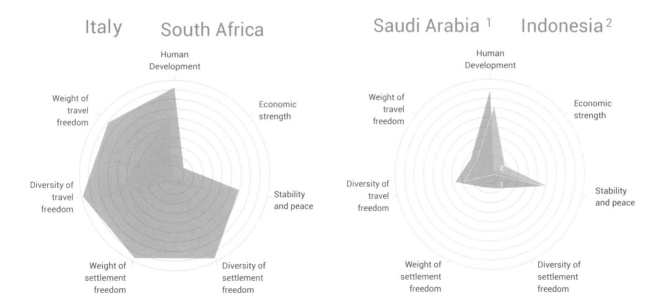

Nationalities of the OECD

	Nationality	Value 2015	Change in value 2014-2015	Change in value 2011-2015	Overall ranking 2015
1	Germany	83.1	0.0	+0.1	1
2	Denmark	83.0	+0.2	+1.7	2
3	Finland	82.0	-0.2	+0.5	3
4	Norway	81.7	+0.5	+0.2	4
5	Iceland	81.6	+0.5	+1.1	5
5	Sweden	81.6	-0.2	+0.2	5
6	Austria	81.0	0.3	+0.2	6
6	Ireland	81.0	-0.2	+0.4	6
7	France	80.9	+0.1	-0.6	7
8	Switzerland	80.7	-0.3	0.0	8
9	Netherlands	80.3	-0.1	+0.4	9
10	Belgium	80.2	-0.2	-0.2	10
11	UK	80.1	-0.1	-0.8	11
12	Spain	79.8	0.0	+0.3	13
12	Italy	79.8	-0.2	-0.4	13
13	Luxembourg	79.3	-0.3	-0.7	14
14	Czech Republic	79.1	+1.0	+6.8	15
15	Portugal	78.9	+0.1	+0.1	16
16	Slovenia	78.8	+0.4	+4.2	17
17	Hungary	78.0	+0.7	+6.8	18
18	Slovakia	77.9	+1.1	+6.5	19
19	Estonia	76.7	+0.9	+7.0	20
19	Poland	76.7	+0.6	+5.0	20
20	Greece	76.5	-0.4	+1.2	21
21	US	63.5	-0.9	-0.3	28
22	Japan	56.2	-1.2	-1.2	30
23	New Zealand	53.4	-0.9	0.0	31
24	Canada	52.7	-0.9	+0.4	32
25	Australia	52.5	-0.7	-0.6	33
26	Chile	52.3	+2.4	+4.0	34
27	Korea (Republic of)	50.8	0.0	+2.6	36
28	Israel	41.9	-0.7	-0.2	49
29	Mexico	39.4	-1.0	-0.8	53
30	Turkey	33.8	+0.8	+1.5	70

Mean: 71.04
Median: 79.0

The Organisation for Economic Co-operation and Development (OECD) was founded in 1961 and consists of 34 highly developed countries. Its members are jointly committed to the promotion of democracy and the free market economy. The OECD provides a platform to discuss trends, best practices and co-ordination in economic, environmental and social policy areas. It had its roots in the Organisation for European Economic Co-operation (OEEC), which was set up in 1948 to administer the Marshall Plan. After its transformation to the OECD, non-European countries were accepted as well.

Members of the OECD are all developed countries with a high level of Human Development and Economic Strength. New global players like the five BRICS countries are not members of the OECD. Because the nationalities of the BRICS countries generally have a medium to low value,[15] the average value of OECD nationalities outperforms any other organization except the EU. Apart from Liechtenstein, the entire top 20 of the QNI General Ranking are also members of the OECD. This results in a whopping mean value of 71.04 (global mean: 38.70) and a median value of 79.0 (world median: 30.90).

In comparison to the other OECD members, Israeli, Mexican and Turkish nationalities have particularly low value. This is mainly the result of a lower level of Stability and Peace, a relatively high number of visa restrictions for passport holders and no Settlement Freedom to other countries.

Most OECD nationalities have consolidated their value over the last five years. New EU Member States have experienced a substantial value increase after intra-EU settlement restrictions for their nationals have been diminished. Chile demonstrates a notable value increase as well, mainly as a result of a mild increase in Settlement Freedom and a significant enhancement of Travel Freedom.

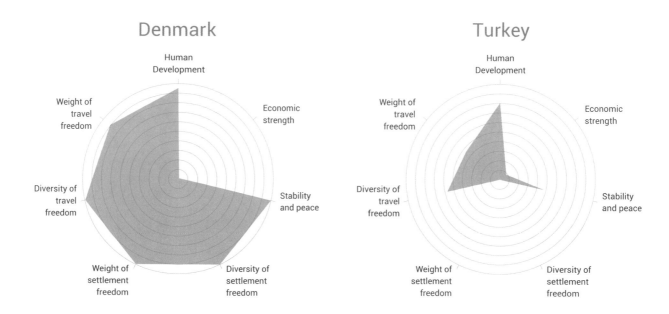

15   See pp 76

Nationalities of BRICS

	Nationality	Value 2015	Change in value 2014-2015	Change in value 2011-2015	Overall ranking 2015
1	Brazil	49.1	-0.3	+1.9	38
2	China	37.4	+0.8	+4.1	60
2	Russian Federation	37.4	+0.6	+3.3	60
3	South Africa	30.0	-0.2	-0.2	89
4	India	27.9	+0.2	+1.4	102

Mean: 36.36
Median: 37.40

BRICS is an association of five newly industrialized and rapidly developing countries: Brazil, the Russian Federation, India, China and South Africa. The former four have been organizing formal diplomatic meetings since 2009. South Africa joined the group in December 2010. The five BRICS countries have a tremendous Economic Strength: their aggregate GDP comprises approximately 20% of world GDP. More importantly, approximately 3 billion people are nationals of one of the BRICS countries; the opportunities and constraints of their nationalities therefore affect almost half of the world's population.

In spite of their significant influence on regional and global developments – both political and economic – the value of BRICS nationalities is below average with a mean value of 36.36 (global mean: 38.70). Not a single one of them is of Very High Quality in QNI terms. The internal value of BRICS nationalities varies greatly: notwithstanding their substantial economic strength, Human Development, and Peace and Stability are generally lower than most western countries. Further, the external value of the BRICS falls short of western nationalities, mainly due to restricted Travel Freedom to many valuable, western-world destinations.

Therefore, the BRICS nationalities occupy medium to low positions on the General QNI Ranking. Short-term and long-term trends vary significantly. While Chinese, Russian and Indian nationalities demonstrate structural quality improvement, South Africa was faced with a mild but persistent decrease.

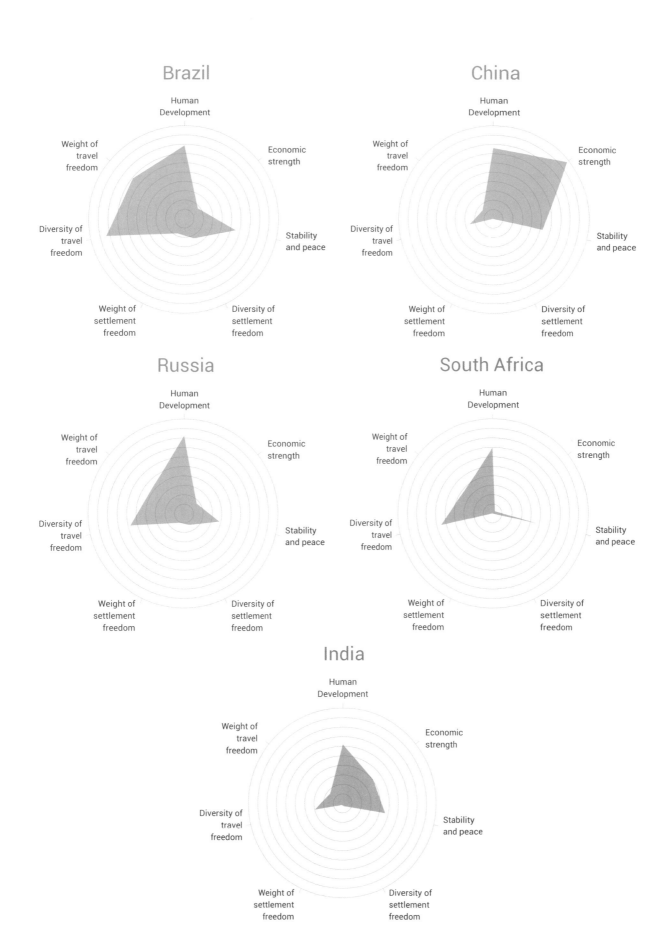

Nationalities of the Commonwealth of Nations

	Nationality	Value 2015	Change in value 2014-2015	Change in value 2011-2015	Overall ranking 2015
1	UK	80.1	-0.1	-0.8	11
2	Malta	76.4	-0.1	+2.8	22
3	Cyprus	73.4	+0.4	+0.6	25
4	New Zealand	53.4	-0.9	0.0	31
5	Canada	52.7	-0.9	+0.4	32
6	Australia	52.5	-0.7	-0.6	33
7	Singapore	51.9	-1.0	+0.2	35
8	Brunei Darussalam	46.5	-1.0	-0.6	43
9	Malaysia	46.3	-0.8	-0.4	44
10	Bahamas	42.5	+0.6	+1.5	48
11	Mauritius	40.6	+0.4	+1.9	50
12	Barbados	39.8	-1.5	-1.0	51
13	Seychelles	38.3	+0.6	+6.1	56
14	Antigua and Barbuda	38.0	-1.4	-0.7	58
15	St. Kitts and Nevis	37.7	-1.5	-0.3	59
16	Trinidad and Tobago	32.6	-0.7	-0.3	78
17	Ghana	32.3	+0.4	-0.1	79
18	St. Lucia	30.3	-1.4	-0.6	86
19	South Africa	30.0	-0.2	-0.2	89
20	St. Vincent and the Grenadines	29.9	-1.6	-0.9	90
21	Grenada	29.8	-0.5	0.0	91
22	Sierra Leone	29.5	+0.4	-4.3	92
23	Dominica	29.3	-1.4	+3.6	93
24	Belize	28.7	-0.9	-1.3	95
25	Maldives	28.5	+0.1	+1.3	96
26	Guyana	28.3	+0.1	+2.2	98
27	Jamaica	28.1	+0.2	-0.1	100
28	Nigeria	28.0	+0.1	-0.4	101
29	India	27.9	+0.1	+1.4	102
30	Botswana	27.6	-1.1	-1.2	104
31	Namibia	26.2	+0.2	+0.4	109
32	Zambia	24.4	+0.1	+0.7	117
33	Lesotho	24.3	+0.4	+0.7	118
34	Papua New Guinea	24.1	+0.3	+0.8	119
35	Swaziland	23.7	+0.3	-0.2	122
36	Kenya	22.7	+0.3	+0.6	128
37	Tanzania	22.6	-0.2	+0.3	129

	Nationality	Value 2015	Change in value 2014-2015	Change in value 2011-2015	Overall ranking 2015
37	Sri Lanka	22.6	+0.2	+0.5	129
38	Malawi	21.9	+0.1	+0.2	132
39	Uganda	21.5	+0.1	+0.6	134
40	Bangladesh	20.2	+0.2	+0.1	138
41	Cameroon	19.3	-0.1	+0.4	146
42	Rwanda	18.9	+0.1	+0.7	148
43	Mozambique	18.8	-0.1	0.0	149
44	Pakistan	17.1	-0.1	-0.6	153

Mean: 34.20
Median: 29.30

The Commonwealth of Nations is an intergovernmental organization formed by 53 countries. They were almost all previously part of the British Empire, except Mozambique, which had been formerly part of Portugal and was admitted to the Commonwealth in 1995. It was created during and after the decolonization, and stands for the common history, language, and values that the members share. The shared values of democracy, human rights protection and the Rule of Law are promoted in the Commonwealth Charter and through the Commonwealth Games. Together, the countries of the Commonwealth of Nations have over 2 billion nationals, or nearly a third of the world population. The nationalities of the Commonwealth of Nations vary greatly in quality, with most of them in the medium-tier of the QNI.

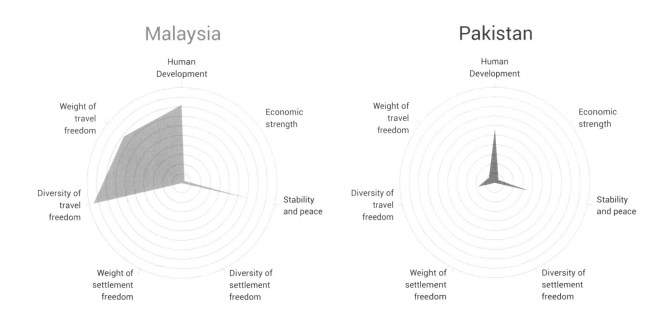

7 Nationalities of Europe

	Nationality	Value 2015	Change in value 2014-2015	Change in value 2011-2015	Overall ranking 2015
1	Germany	83.1	0	+0.1	1
2	Denmark	83.0	+0.2	+1.7	2
3	Finland	82.0	-0.2	+0.5	3
4	Norway	81.7	+0.5	+0.2	4
5	Sweden	81.6	-0.1	+0.2	5
5	Iceland	81.6	+0.5	+1.1	5
6	Ireland	81.0	-0.2	+0.3	6
6	Austria	81.0	+0.3	+0.1	6
7	France	80.9	+0.1	-0.6	7
8	Switzerland	80.7	-0.3	0.0	8
9	Netherlands	80.3	-0.1	+0.4	9
10	Belgium	80.2	-0.2	-0.2	10
11	UK	80.1	-0.1	-0.8	11
12	Liechtenstein	80.0	-0.1	+0.2	12
13	Italy	79.8	-0.2	-0.4	13
13	Spain	79.8	0.0	+0.2	13
14	Luxembourg	79.3	-0.3	-0.8	14
15	Czech Republic	79.1	+1.0	+6.8	15
16	Portugal	78.9	+0.1	+0.1	16
17	Slovenia	78.8	+0.4	+4.2	17
18	Hungary	78.0	+0.7	+6.8	18
19	Slovakia	77.9	+1.1	+6.5	19
20	Estonia	76.7	+1.0	+7.0	20
20	Poland	76.7	+0.6	+5.0	20
21	Greece	76.5	-0.4	+1.2	21
22	Malta	76.4	-0.1	+2.8	22
23	Lithuania	76.2	+0.9	+6.2	23
24	Latvia	76.0	+0.7	+7.1	24
25	Cyprus	73.4	+0.4	+0.7	25
26	Romania	72.6	+9.8	+13.6	26
27	Bulgaria	72.4	+10.2	+14.2	27
	(European Union)	67.5	-0.6	-1.0	n/a
28	Croatia	58.3	+2.5	+17.5	29
29	San Marino	48.5	-0.8	+0.1	39

	Nationality	Value 2015	Change in value 2014-2015	Change in value 2011-2015	Overall ranking 2015
30	Monaco	48.4	-0.6	-0.9	40
31	Andorra	47.0	-1.1	-0.3	42
32	Russian Federation	37.4	+0.6	+3.3	60
33	Serbia	35.8	-0.2	+1.9	64
34	Montenegro	34.6	-0.6	+0.5	65
35	Macedonia	34.4	+0.1	+1.3	66
36	Turkey	33.8	0.8	1.5	70
37	Bosnia and Herzegovina	33.3	+0.1	+6.5	74
38	Moldova	32.7	+4.1	+4.6	77
39	Albania	32.0	-0.3	+6.3	80
40	Belarus	31.6	-0.6	+0.6	82
41	Ukraine	30.2	-2.2	+0.2	87
42	Georgia	27.8	+0.9	+2.3	103
43	Azerbaijan	27.1	-1.4	-0.1	107
44	(Non-citizen) Latvia	26.2	0.0	+0.4	109
45	Armenia	26.1	-1.7	-0.7	110
46	Kosovo	23.8	+0.3	+1.4	121

Mean: 62.79
Median: 76.50

The quality of European nationalities far exceeds the global average. In 2015, the top 32 nationalities were all European. The mean of all 49 European nationalities was 62.79 (global mean: 38.70) and its median was 76.50 (global median: 30.90). This average is unmatched by any other region and only surpassed by the OECD nationalities.

Most prominently are the nationalities of the EU Member States. Passport holders of any of the EU Member States enjoy an unprecedented external value of nationality. The non-EU European nationalities have considerable lower external value, which is directly visible in their overall values.

Over the past five years, the new EU Member States, which acceded to the EU in 2004 and 2007, experienced the greatest increase in value. In 2010, their nationals were still significantly restricted with regards to free settlement in other EU Member States. In 2014, the last restrictions were lifted so that the nationals of the new EU Member States had full access throughout the EU. It must be noted, however, that a substantial number of inhabitants of Latvia possess the Latvian non-citizen status, which does not grant them free movement rights.

Because the cut-off date for the 2015 Settlement Freedom is set at 31 December 2015, the nationality of Croatia will continue to gain value of the next years as settlement restrictions to other EU Member States will be lifted.

Meanwhile, the old EU Member States have maintained their top positions, and have experienced only minor fluctuations in value. They generally possess a higher internal value than the non-EU and new EU Member States. Moreover, Travel Freedom Diversity is generally higher as well. For example, passports of Germany, Finland, Sweden and the UK provide visa-free or visa on arrival access to 174 destinations, and other western European nationalities follow closely. The highest ranking new EU Member States are Czech Republic and Hungary with 'only' 162 destinations.

Outside the EU, notable examples are Bosnia and Herzegovina, and Albania, which saw substantial value increases in the past five years. The Travel Freedom Diversity of Bosnia and Herzegovina raised from 53 visa-free or visa on arrival destinations in 2011 to 95 in 2015. Similarly, nationals of Albania enjoyed an increase in Travel Freedom Diversity from 49 destinations in 2011 to 91 in 2015.

The nationality of Kosovo has the lowest value due to weaknesses in both Internal and External Value. Nonetheless, its current value is still somewhat inflated because the QNI does not directly take into account the fact that Kosovan nationality is not recognized by a number of countries.

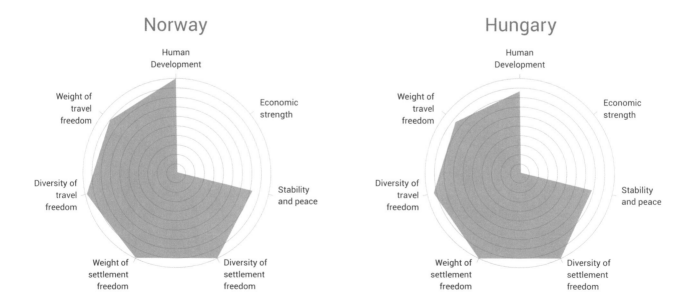

Bosnia and Herzegovina

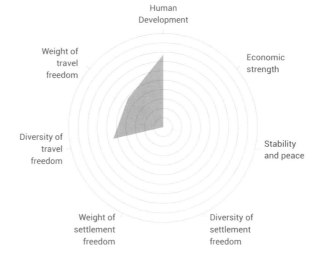

Kosovo

8   Nationalities of the Americas

Nationalities of North America

	Nationality	Value 2015	Change in value 2014-2015	Change in value 2011-2015	Overall ranking 2015
1	The US	63.5	-1.0	-0.4	28
2	Canada	52.7	-0.9	+0.4	32

Mean: 58.1
Median: 58.1

The nationalities of North America remain fairly stable and follow the EU Member States in the very high quality tier of the QNI. Last year, both nationalities lost some value due to the introduction of restricted settlement access in Georgia. Over the past five years, however, both US and Canadian nationality roughly maintained their value and ranking.

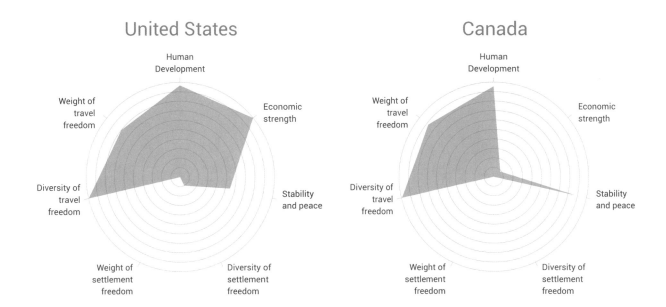

Nationalities of Central America and the Caribbean

	Nationality	Value 2015	Change in value 2014-2015	Change in value 2011-2015	Overall ranking 2015
1	Bahamas	42.5	+0.6	+1.5	48
2	Barbados	39.8	-1.5	-1.0	51
3	Mexico	39.4	-1.0	-0.8	53
4	Costa Rica	39.1	-0.4	-1.0	54
5	Panama	38.1	-0.6	+1.4	57
6	Antigua and Barbuda	38.0	-1.4	-0.7	58
7	St. Kitts and Nevis	37.7	-1.5	-0.3	59
8	El Salvador	34.0	-1.5	-1.1	68
9	Guatemala	33.9	-1.0	-0.6	69
10	Honduras	33.6	-0.6	0.0	72
11	Nicaragua	33.1	+0.1	+0.5	76
12	Trinidad and Tobago	32.6	-0.7	-0.3	78
13	St. Lucia	30.3	-1.4	-0.6	86
14	St. Vincent and the Grenadines	29.9	-1.6	-0.9	90
15	Grenada	29.8	-0.5	0.0	91
16	Dominica	29.3	-1.4	+3.6	93
17	Belize	28.7	-0.9	-1.3	95
18	Jamaica	28.1	+0.2	-0.1	100
19	Cuba	27.3	-1.1	+0.1	106
20	Dominican Republic	24.8	-0.8	-3.6	114
21	Haiti	20.0	+0.1	+1.1	140

Mean: 32.86
Median: 33.10

The nationalities of Central America and the Caribbean are invariably in the medium to high quality tiers of the QNI. There exist quite substantial differences between the top-ranked nationalities of the region, which are in the top 60 of the QNI General Ranking, and the less valued nationalities, falling outside the top 100. Such variety is present in the entire range of elements; with higher-scoring nationalities having generally stronger economies, higher development and more stability and peace, but also benefiting from greater Travel Freedom. However, the general lack of significant Settlement Freedom prevents even the top-ranked nationalities in this region from matching the European, North American and some of the East Asian nationalities.

Nationalities of South America

	Nationality	Value 2015	Change in value 2014-2015	Change in value 2011-2015	Overall ranking 2015
1	Chile	52.3	+2.4	+4.0	34
2	Argentina	50.4	+0.7	+2.3	37
3	Brazil	49.1	-0.3	+1.9	38
4	Uruguay	47.7	-0.2	+2.0	41
5	Paraguay	42.7	+0.2	+1.4	47
6	Venezuela	39.0	0.0	+0.7	55
7	Peru	36.5	+0.4	+2.0	61
8	Ecuador	34.3	+5.1	+6.5	67
9	Bolivia	33.7	+0.4	+2.4	71
10	Colombia	31.7	+0.2	+6.6	81
11	Suriname	28.8	-0.3	+1.2	94
12	Guyana	28.3	+0.1	+2.2	98

Mean: 39.54
Median: 37.75

The South America region comprises 12 nationalities, which are largely in the high to medium quality tier of the QNI. The continent is currently experiencing far-reaching economic integration particularly among the Member States of MERCOSUR. As a result, the regional mean (39.54) is slightly higher than the global mean (38.70) and the regional median (37.75) even substantially higher than the global one (30.90).

Among the South American nationalities, full members of MERCOSUR outperform other nationalities of the continent as a result of their higher level of economic integration and stronger economic development. However, some of the other nationalities, in particular Ecuador and Colombia, have seen spectacular increases in quality over the past five years. These steep rises in quality have to do with a serious extension of free movement, residence and working rights abroad. As of 31 December 2014, the cut-off date for the 2015 Settlement Freedom data, Ecuadorians can work in Argentina, Brazil, Colombia, Bolivia, Peru, Uruguay and Paraguay. Earlier, Chilean nationals acquired full access to Bolivia, Brazil, Paraguay, and Uruguay.

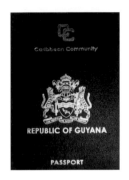

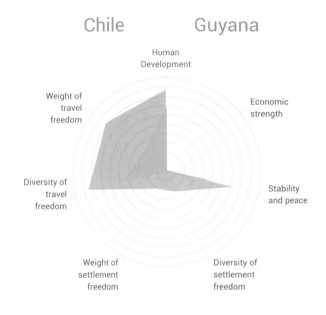

Chile   Guyana

Human
Development

Weight of   Economic
travel   strength
freedom

Diversity of   Stability
travel   and peace
freedom

Weight of   Diversity of
settlement   settlement
freedom   freedom

Venezuela   Ecuador

Human
Development

Weight of   Economic
travel   strength
freedom

Diversity of   Stability
travel   and peace
freedom

Weight of   Diversity of
settlement   settlement
freedom   freedom

9 Nationalities of the Middle East and North Africa

	Nationality	Value 2015	Change in value 2014-2015	Change in value 2011-2015	Overall ranking 2015
1	Israel	41.9	-0.7	-0.2	49
2	Qatar	37.4	-0.3	-0.7	60
3	United Arab Emirates	36.3	-0.2	+0.2	62
4	Kuwait	36.0	-0.8	-0.8	63
5	Saudi Arabia	34.0	-0.6	+0.9	68
6	Oman	33.4	-0.5	-2.0	73
7	Bahrain	33.2	-1.2	-2.1	75
8	Tunisia	26.9	+0.1	-1.2	108
9	Jordan	24.3	0.0	+0.4	118
10	Morocco	23.8	+0.4	+0.1	121
11	Algeria	23.3	-0.2	-0.2	124
12	Iran	22.8	-0.2	+0.4	127
13	Egypt	22.6	-0.6	-1.2	129
14	Libya	22.5	0.0	-2.4	130
15	Lebanon	22.0	-0.1	-0.1	131
16	Palestinian Territory	19.9	-0.2	+0.6	141
17	Yemen	18.4	0.0	+0.6	150
18	Iraq	18.0	-1.2	-0.2	151
19	Syria	17.3	-2.1	-4.2	152
20	Sudan	16.1	-0.3	+1.0	157

Mean: 32.86
Median: 33.10

The Middle East and North Africa largely consist of medium to low valued nationalities. The mean of the region lies at 26.85, which is substantially below the global mean of 38.70. Within the region, there is great divergence between the upper performers, including Israel and Saudi Arabia, and the lowest-scoring nationalities, including statuses attached to (civil) war-torn countries such as Iraq and Syria.

External value is generally low and Settlement Freedom for many nationalities even non-existent. Nationalities associated with Member States of the Gulf Cooperation Council however enjoy Settlement Freedom in the other five Member States. Together with Israel these nationalities consequently outperform the other Middle Eastern and Northern African nationalities by far. After the nationalities of Israel and the six Gulf Cooperation Council countries, the next nationality follows at 7.2 points and 33 ranks distance.

Qatar   Iraq

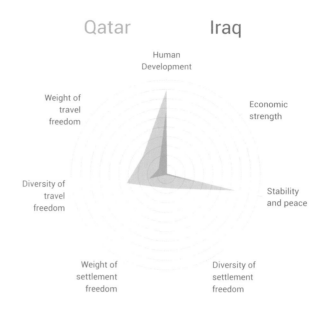

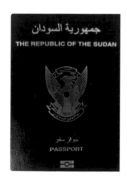

Israel   Sudan

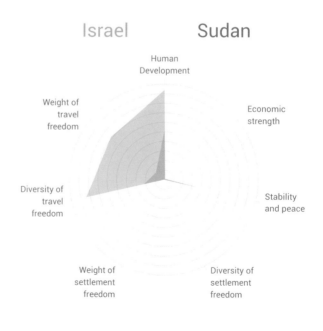

10 Nationalities of Sub-Saharan Africa

	Nationality	Value 2015	Change in value 2014-2015	Change in value 2011-2015	Overall ranking 2015
1	Mauritius	40.6	+0.4	+1.9	50
2	Seychelles	38.3	+0.6	+6.1	56
3	Cape Verde	32.7	0.0	+1.2	77
4	Ghana	32.3	+0.4	-0.1	79
5	Gambia	30.7	+0.3	-0.4	84
6	Benin	30.4	+0.5	+0.9	85
7	Senegal	30.1	+0.4	+1.0	88
8	South Africa	30.0	-0.2	-0.2	89
9	Sierra Leone	29.5	+0.4	-4.3	92
10	Togo	29.3	+0.1	+0.6	93
11	Côte d'Ivoire	28.4	+0.7	+0.5	97
12	Burkina Faso	28.2	+0.5	+0.4	99
13	Nigeria	28.0	+0.1	-0.4	101
14	Liberia	27.8	+0.6	+1.1	103
14	Mali	27.8	0.0	+0.3	103
15	Botswana	27.6	-1.1	-1.2	104
15	Guinea	27.6	+0.1	+0.1	104
16	Niger	26.9	+0.3	+1.0	108
17	Guinea-Bissau	26.2	0.0	-0.1	109
17	Namibia	26.2	+0.2	+0.4	109
18	Zambia	24.4	+0.1	+0.7	117
19	Lesotho	24.3	+0.4	+0.7	118
20	Swaziland	23.7	+0.3	-0.2	122
21	Gabon	23.0	0.0	+0.7	125
22	Kenya	22.7	+0.3	+0.6	128
23	Tanzania	22.6	-0.2	+0.3	129
24	Malawi	21.9	+0.1	+0.2	132
25	Sao Tome and Principe	21.6	0.0	+0.7	133
26	Uganda	21.5	+0.1	+0.6	134
27	Zimbabwe	20.7	+0.1	+0.7	136
28	Madagascar	20.5	+0.3	+0.6	137
29	Mauritania	20.1	-0.4	+0.3	139
30	Equatorial Guinea	20.0	-0.2	0.0	140
31	**Congo**	**19.8**	**-0.4**	**-0.4**	**142**

	Nationality	Value 2015	Change in value 2014-2015	Change in value 2011-2015	Overall ranking 2015
32	Comoros	19.5	0.0	+0.5	144
33	Angola	19.4	0.0	+0.7	145
34	Cameroon	19.3	-0.1	+0.4	146
35	Djibouti	19.1	-0.1	-0.4	147
36	Rwanda	18.9	+0.1	+0.7	148
37	Mozambique	18.8	-0.1	0.0	149
38	Ethiopia	17.0	-0.2	+1.0	154
39	Chad	16.8	-0.2	+1.4	155
40	Burundi	16.7	+0.3	+0.9	156
41	Eritrea	15.9	-0.2	+0.3	158
42	Central African Republic	15.3	-0.7	-1.7	159
43	Congo (Democratic Republic of the)	14.3	-0.3	+0.3	161

Mean: 24.27
Median: 23.35

The Sub-Saharan African nationalities on average have the second to lowest value just above South Asia, with a mean of 24.27 and a median of 23.35. No nationality ranks in the top 50. The nationalities of the Seychelles and Mauritius score substantially higher than other Sub-Saharan African statuses, mainly because of their relatively high Travel Freedom Diversity: 126 and 125 destinations respectively.

Generally, the Sub-Saharan African nationalities suffer from weaknesses in both internal and external value. Low levels of Human Development, Economic Strength and Stability and Peace and combined with high restrictions on Travel Freedom and marginal or no Settlement Freedom. However, Member States of the ECOWAS benefit from a significant level of economic integration. As a result, their value is clearly distinguishable due to the free movement rights for their nationals. Nonetheless, discriminatory policies are still in place in some countries, particular sectors are still excluded to foreign workers, and the level of Settlement Freedom is incomparable to that of, for example, the EU.[16]

16 See below pp 94, and generally A Devillard, A Bacchi and M Noack, A Survey on Migration Policies in West Africa (International Centre for Migration Policy Development and International Organization for Migration 2015)

11   Nationalities of Asia and the Pacific

	Nationality	Value 2015	Change in value 2014-2015	Change in value 2011-2015	Overall ranking 2015
1	Japan	56.2	-1.2	-1.2	30
2	New Zealand	53.4	-0.9	0.0	31
3	Australia	52.5	-0.7	-0.6	33
4	Singapore	51.9	-1.0	+0.2	35
5	Korea (Republic of)	50.8	0.0	+2.6	36
6	Brunei Darussalam	46.5	-1.0	-0.6	43
7	Malaysia	46.3	-0.8	-0.4	44
8	Hong Kong. China (SAR)	44.4	-0.2	+0.3	45
9	Taiwa	44.0	0.0	+13.1	46
10	Macao	39.5	+0.4	+2.2	52
11	China	37.4	+0.8	+4.1	60
12	Kazakhstan	31.1	+0.5	+2.9	83
13	Maldives	28.5	+0.1	+1.3	96
14	Thailand	28.0	-1.0	+0.7	101
15	India	27.9	+0.1	+1.4	102
16	Indonesia	27.4	+0.3	+1.9	105
17	Uzbekistan	25.4	-1.5	-0.9	111
18	Philippines	25.2	+0.2	+1.5	112
19	Mongolia	25.0	+0.5	+1.9	113
20	Bhutan	24.7	+0.3	+2.3	115
21	Tajikistan	24.6	-1.0	-1.2	116
22	Kyrgyzstan	24.1	-1.7	-1.5	119
22	Papua New Guinea	24.1	+0.3	+0.8	119
23	Vietnam	24.0	+0.3	+1.1	120
24	Turkmenistan	23.4	-0.4	+0.3	123
25	Laos	22.9	+0.2	+1.1	126
25	Timor-Leste	22.9	-0.1	+0.8	126
26	Sri Lanka	22.6	+0.2	+0.5	129
27	Cambodia	22.0	+0.3	+2.0	131
28	Nepal	20.9	0.0	0.0	135
29	Bangladesh	20.2	+0.2	+0.1	138
30	Myanmar	19.7	+0.3	+1.8	143
31	Pakistan	17.1	-0.1	-0.6	153
32	Afghanistan	14.4	-0.1	+0.2	160

Mean: 31.44
Median: 25.30

Asian nationalities occupy positions in the entire spectrum of the QNI, from the very high quality tier (Japan, New Zealand, Australia, Singapore, and South Korea) to the low quality tier (Myanmar, Pakistan, and Afghanistan). The majority of Asian nationalities have a medium quality. With a mean of 31.44 and a median of 25.30, the region scores below the global average.

Asian nationalities generally score low on Settlement Freedom, which leaves them invariably outside the top ranks. The wide variety in quality among the Asian nationalities is caused by substantial differences in Internal Value and Travel Freedom. East and Southeast Asian nationalities generally score higher on Human Development, Economic Strength and Stability and Peace than the nationalities of Eurasia and South Asia. Moreover, they also benefit from a superior number of visa-free or visa on arrival travel destinations.

The nationalities of New Zealand and Australia are both in the very high quality tier of the QNI. Nationals of these countries enjoy excellent Travel Freedom, having visa-free or visa on arrival tourist and business access to 170 (New Zealand) and 168 (Australia) destinations. Further, both Australia and New Zealand grant full access to each other's nationals.

The most notable rise in quality has been experienced by the nationality of Taiwan. This is mainly caused by a spectacular rise in Travel Freedom, from 60 visa-free or visa on arrival destinations in 2011 to 132 destinations in 2015. In particular the abolishment of visa requirements for access to the Schengen area contributed to this effect. As China announced the lifting of visa restrictions in 2015 after the cut-off date of 1 May 2015, the value of Taiwanese nationality is likely to improve further in 2016.

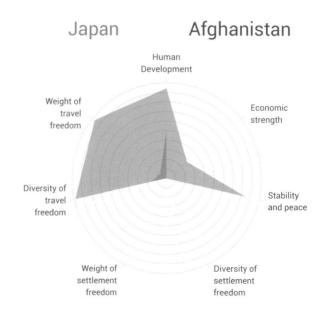

12 Regional blocs and organizations

Nationalities of the European Union

	Nationality	Value 2015	Change in value 2014-2015	Change in value 2011-2015	Overall ranking 2015
1	Germany	83.1	0	+0.1	1
2	Denmark	83.0	+0.2	+1.7	2
3	Finland	82.0	-0.2	+0.5	3
4	Sweden	81.6	-0.1	+0.2	5
5	Ireland	81.0	-0.2	+0.3	6
5	Austria	81.0	+0.3	+0.1	6
6	France	80.9	+0.1	-0.6	7
7	Netherlands	80.3	-0.1	+0.4	9
8	Belgium	80.2	-0.2	-0.2	10
9	UK	80.1	-0.1	-0.8	11
10	Italy	79.8	-0.2	-0.4	13
10	Spain	79.8	0.0	+0.2	13
11	Luxembourg	79.3	-0.3	-0.8	14
12	Czech Republic	79.1	+1.0	+6.8	15
13	Portugal	78.9	+0.1	+0.1	16
14	Slovenia	78.8	+0.4	+4.2	17
15	Hungary	78.0	+0.7	+6.8	18
16	Slovakia	77,9	+1.1	+6.5	19
17	Estonia	76.7	+1.0	+7.0	20
17	Poland	76.7	+0.6	+5.0	20
18	Greece	76.5	-0.4	+1.2	21
19	Malta	76.4	-0.1	+2.8	22
20	Lithuania	76.2	+0.9	+6.2	23
21	Latvia	76.0	+0.7	+7.1	24
22	Cyprus	73.4	+0.4	+0.7	25
23	Romania	72.6	+9.8	+13.6	26
24	Bulgaria	72.4	+10.2	+14.2	27
	(European Union)	67.5	-0.6	-1.0	n/a
25	Croatia	58.3	+2.5	+17.5	29
26	(Non-citizen) Latvia	26.2	0.0	+0.4	109

Mean: 76.46
Median: 78.85

The EU, founded in 1957, is a political and economic union of currently 28 Member States. It aims at creating an 'ever closer union' between the peoples of Europe, and has to that end achieved extensive and deep economic integration. The EU comprises an internal market in which all obstacles to the free movement of goods, services, persons and capital are prohibited. Moreover, nationals of the EU Member States are also 'EU citizens', which allows them to travel and settle freely in other Member States.

Because of the unprecedented level of economic integration, the quality of EU nationalities is unmatched. All nationalities of the EU are in the very high quality tier of the QNI, except for the status of non-citizens in Latvia, who have no EU free movement rights. The relatively high ranking of Latvian nationality must in this light be nuanced, as a significant number of Latvian inhabitants possess only the non-citizen status.

Moreover, the top 27 nationalities are all attached to EU Member States. The value of EU citizenship is unambiguously illustrated by the accession of new Member States, including Romania, Bulgaria and Croatia. Their nationalities have experienced a massive increase in quality following their states' integration in the EU.

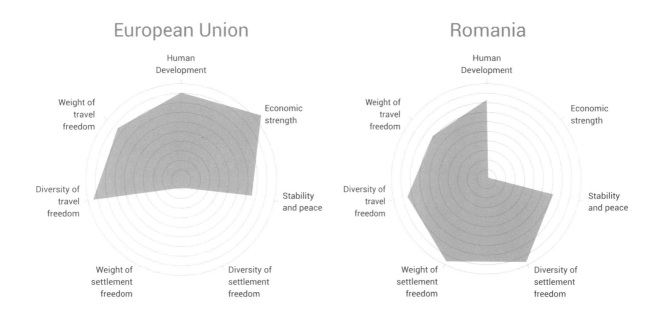

Nationalities of the CIS

	Nationality	Value 2015	Change in value 2014-2015	Change in value 2011-2015	Overall ranking 2015
1	Russian Federation	37.4	+0.6	+3.3	60
2	Moldova	32.7	+4.1	+4.6	77
3	Belarus	31.6	-0.6	+0.6	82
4	Kazakhstan	31.1	+0.5	+2.9	83
5	Azerbaijan	27.1	-1.4	-0.1	107
6	Armenia	;26.1	-1.7	-0.7	110
7	Uzbekistan	25.4	-1.5	-0.9	111
8	Tajikistan	24.6	-1.0	-1.2	116
9	Kyrgyzstan	24.1	-1.7	-1.5	119

Mean: 28.90
Median: 27.10

The Commonwealth of Independent States (CIS) consists of nine countries that were former republics of the Soviet Union. They form a loose intergovernmental organization focused on trade and finance cooperation. Moreover, five of the CIS countries have recently founded the Eurasian Economic Union, a full economic union comprised of Armenia, Belarus, Kazakhstan, Kyrgyzstan, and Russia.

Most nationalities of the CIS countries are in the medium quality tier of the QNI, with Russia standing out in the lower range of the high quality tier. Over the past years, the nationality of Moldova saw the greatest increase in value. This increase was predominantly the result of 32 additional visa-free or visa on arrival travel destinations over the past five years.

Until 2014, Russia gave de facto full access to nationals of the CIS countries.[17] This was a major boost for the quality of the CIS nationalities, as it positively affected the settlement opportunities these nationals had in light of Russia's Economic Strength. Russia's tighter policy entailed that only nationals of Belarus and Kazakhstan continued to have full access as of 31 December 2014 – the cut-off date for 2015 Settlement Freedom – while the other CIS nationalities incurred negative effects on Settlement Freedom and Overall Value.

However, in 2015, Russia announced future full access for all nationals of the Eurasia Economic Union Member States. Accordingly, in addition to continuing full access of Belarus and Kazakhstan, nationals of Armenia and Kyrgyzstan will receive full access to Russia in the near future. The nationalities of Armenia and Kyrgyzstan will, therefore, see further quality increases in 2016 and 2017.

17 See the special contribution by Greg Nizhnikaŭ, 'The Commonwealth of Independent States Region', pp 143

Nationalities of the ASEAN

	Nationality	Value 2015	Change in value 2014-2015	Change in value 2011-2015	Overall ranking 2015
1	Singapore	51.9	-1.0	+0.2	35
2	Brunei Darussalam	46.5	-1.0	-0.6	43
3	Malaysia	46.3	-0.8	-0.4	44
4	Thailand	28.0	-1.0	+0.7	101
5	Indonesia	27.4	+0.3	+1.9	105
6	Philippines	25.2	+0.2	+1.5	112
7	Vietnam	24.0	+0.3	+1.1	120
8	Laos	22.9	+0.2	+1.1	126
9	Cambodia	22.0	+0.3	+2.0	131
10	Myanmar	19.7	0.3	1.8	143

Mean: 31.39
Median: 26.30

The Association of Southeast Asian Nations (ASEAN) is a political and economic organization of 10 Southeast Asian countries. It was founded in 1967 and has since then focused on *inter alia* economic cooperation and maintaining regional peace and stability. In 2007, the Member States signed the ASEAN Charter, in which they agreed to deepen economic integration to create an 'EU-style community'. While nationals do not yet enjoy genuine settlement freedom in the other Member States, it is the ambition of the ASEAN Member States to create full freedom of workers in the near future.

The ASEAN nationalities vary widely in quality. The nationalities of Singapore, Brunei Darussalam and Malaysia are far superior than the others and the only ones in the top 100. These nationalities benefit from stronger economies, a higher level of human development and more peacefulness. Moreover, they also outperform the other Member States on External Value, having visa-free or visa on arrival travel freedom to over 140 destinations.

Nationalities of MERCOSUR

	Nationality	Value 2015	Change in value 2014-2015	Change in value 2011-2015	Overall ranking 2015
1	Argentina	50.4	+0.7	+2.3	37
2	Brazil	49.1	-0.3	+1.9	38
3	Uruguay	47.7	-0.2	+2.0	41
4	Paraguay	42.7	+0.2	+1.4	47
5	Venezuela	39.0	0.0	+0.7	55

Mean: 45.78
Median: 47.70

The MERCOSUR (Mercado Común del Sur, or Southern Common Market) is a regional trade organization composed of six Member States: Argentina, Brazil, Paraguay, Uruguay, Venezuela and Bolivia, which joined last year and will be reflected in QNI 2016. The organization was created in 1991 and aspires to free movement of goods, services and persons among its members, with the future aim of full economic integration. It currently has six associate members – Chile, Peru, Colombia, Ecuador, Guyana and Suriname – which benefit from partial integration in the economic area.

MERCOSUR is currently the 4th largest economy in the world, after the EU, the North American Free Trade Agreement (NAFTA), and the Association of South East Asian Nations (ASEAN). Together, its Member States count over 270 million nationals.

The nationalities of MERCOSUR are in the high to very high quality tier of the QNI, Argentina standing out with just over 50%. Because nationals can genuinely enjoy free movement and full access throughout the economic area, both External Value and Overall Ranking are substantially higher than most other Latin American nationalities.

Argentina   Venezuela

Nationalities of the Gulf Cooperation Council

	Nationality	Value 2015	Change in value 2014-2015	Change in value 2011-2015	Overall ranking 2015
1	Qatar	37.4	-0.3	-0.7	60
2	United Arab Emirates	36.3	-0.2	+0.2	62
3	Kuwait	36.0	-0.8	-0.8	63
4	Saudi Arabia	34.0	-0.6	+0.9	68
5	Oman	33.4	-0.5	-2.0	73
6	Bahrain	33.2	-1.2	-2.1	75

Mean: 35.05
Median: 35.00

The Gulf Cooperation Council (GCC) is a political and economic union between six Arab countries surrounding the Persian Gulf. It was founded in 1981 and aims to foster cooperation on a number of economic and policy issues, including harmonizing regulation, technological and industrial progress, strengthening ties between nations and a common currency.

The nationals of the GCC enjoy free movement rights and can therefore freely settle in the other countries. However, unlike most other countries, the GCC countries have no clear overlap between inhabitants and nationals: the overwhelming majority of workforce are non-nationals. Nationals therefore make very little use of their Settlement Freedom to work in the other GCC countries.

The nationalities of the GCC have a high to medium quality of nationality. As a result of regional instability, the quality of some nationalities has decreased somewhat over the last five years. The large economies of the oil-producing states and their relatively high level of human development are combined with relatively high External Value.

Nationalities of the Arab League

	Nationality	Value 2015	Change in value 2014-2015	Change in value 2011-2015	Overall ranking 2015
1	Qatar	37.4	-0.3	-0.7	60
2	United Arab Emirates	36.3	-0.2	+0.2	62
3	Kuwait	36.0	-0.8	-0.8	63
4	Saudi Arabia	34.0	-0.6	+0.9	68
5	Oman	33.4	-0.5	-2.0	73
6	Bahrain	33.2	-1.2	-2.1	75
7	Tunisia	26.9	+0.1	-1.2	108
8	Jordan	24.3	0.0	+0.4	118
9	Morocco	23.8	+0.4	+0.1	121
10	Algeria	23.3	-0.2	-0.2	124
11	Egypt	22.6	-0.6	-1.2	129
12	Libya	22.5	0.0	-2.4	130
13	Lebanon	22.0	-0.1	-0.1	131
14	Mauritania	20.1	-0.4	+0.3	139
15	Palestinian Territory	19.9	-0.2	+0.6	141
16	Comoros	19.5	0.0	+0.5	144
17	Djibouti	19.1	-0.1	-0.4	147
18	Yemen	18.4	0.0	+0.6	150
19	Iraq	18.0	-1.2	-0.2	151
20	Syria	17.3	-2.1	-4.2	152
21	Sudan	16.1	-0.3	+1.0	157

Mean: 24.96
Median: 22.60

The Arab League is a regional organization of Arab countries in Northern Africa, the Horn of Africa and the Arabian Peninsula. It is comprised of 22 Member States,[18] of which all but Somalia are represented in the QNI. The Arab League has no supranational powers and functions mainly as a platform to discuss and coordinate policy issues, common interests and concerns, and solve conflicts among its members.

The nationalities of the Arab League are predominantly in the medium to low quality tiers of the QNI. The Gulf Cooperation Council nationalities clearly stand out in quality because of their superior economic size and the free movement rights of their nationals. Regional instability has had detrimental effects on Human Development and Stability and Peace, which particularly affected the quality of Libyan, Egyptian and Syrian nationalities.

18 Although Syria's membership has been suspended since 2011 because of the Government's repression of the uprising and the civil war

Nationalities of the ECOWAS

	Nationality	Value 2015	Change in value 2014-2015	Change in value 2011-2015	Overall ranking 2015
1	Cape Verde	32.7	0.0	+1.2	77
2	Ghana	32.3	+0.4	-0.1	89
3	Gambia	30.7	+0.3	-0.4	84
4	Benin	30.4	+0.5	+0.9	85
5	Senegal	30.1	+0.4	+1.0	88
6	Sierra Leone	29.5	+0.4	-4.3	92
7	Togo	29.3	+0.1	+0.6	93
8	Côte d'Ivoire	28.4	+0.7	+0.5	97
9	Burkina Faso	28.2	+0.5	+0.4	99
10	Nigeria	28.0	+0.1	-0.4	101
11	Liberia	27.8	+0.6	+1.1	103
11	Mali	27.8	0.0	+0.3	103
12	Guinea	27.6	+0.1	+0.1	104
13	Niger	26.9	+0.3	+1.0	108
14	Guinea-Bissau	26.2	0.0	-0.1	109

Mean: 29.06
Median: 28.40

The Economic Community of West African States (ECOWAS) is a regional organization in West Africa primarily aimed at creating collective self-sufficiency for its members. It was founded in 1975 and consists of 15 Member States. The ECOWAS is focused on free trade and the nationals of its members are largely entitled to full access in the other countries. Nevertheless, discriminatory policies are still in place in some countries, which restrict access of foreign workers to particular sectors.[19] Cape Verde and Benin do not give general full access to foreign ECOWAS nationals.

The ECOWAS nationalities are in the medium quality tier of the QNI. Although their value is substantially higher than other Sub-Saharan African nationalities, their overall ranking lags behind nationalities of the developed world. Generally, the quality of ECOWAS nationalities remains stable despite high economic growth numbers. The nationality of Sierra Leone however experienced a notable value decrease in the past five years, mainly due to newly introduced visa restrictions for 48 travel destinations.

19 See A Devillard, A Bacchi and M Noack, A Survey on Migration Policies in West Africa (International Centre for Migration Policy Development and International Organization for Migration 2015), for example: 'Ghana legally restricts the employment of foreigners in certain sectors (marketplace trading, petty trading, hawking, kiosk trade, operation of taxi and car hire services, pool betting, and operation of beauty salons and barber shops). In Mali, the restricted sectors are health, law, and public services' (46–47)

Nationalities of NATO

	Nationality	Value 2015	Change in value 2014-2015	Change in value 2011-2015	Overall ranking 2015
1	Germany	83.1	0	+0.1	1
2	Denmark	83.0	+0.2	+1.7	2
3	Norway	81.7	+0.5	+0.2	4
4	Iceland	81.6	+0.5	+1.1	5
5	France	80.9	+0.1	-0.6	7
6	Netherlands	80.3	-0.1	+0.4	9
7	Belgium	80.2	-0.2	-0.2	10
8	UK	80.1	-0.1	-0.8	11
9	Italy	79.8	-0.2	-0.4	13
9	Spain	79.8	0.0	+0.2	13
10	Luxembourg	79.3	-0.3	-0.8	14
11	Czech Republic	79.1	+1.0	+6.8	15
12	Portugal	78.9	+0.1	+0.1	16
13	Slovenia	78.8	+0.4	+4.2	17
14	Hungary	78.0	+0.7	+6.8	18
15	Slovakia	77.9	+1.1	+6.5	19
16	Estonia	76.7	+1.0	+7.0	20
16	Poland	76.7	+0.6	+5.0	20
17	Greece	76.5	-0.4	+1.2	21
18	Lithuania	76.2	+0.9	+6.2	23
19	Latvia	76.0	+0.7	+7.1	24
20	Romania	72.6	+9.8	+13.6	26
21	Bulgaria	72.4	+10.2	+14.2	27
22	US	63.5	-1.0	-0.4	28
23	Croatia	58.3	+2.5	+17.5	29
24	Canada	52.7	-0.9	+0.4	32
25	Turkey	33.8	+0.8	+1.5	70
26	Albania	32.0	-0.3	+6.3	80
27	(Non-citizen) Latvia	26.2	0.0	+0.4	109

Mean: 71.93
Median: 78.00

The North Atlantic Treaty Organization (NATO) is a post-WWII intergovernmental military organization based on collective defense. It was set up in 1949 and played a major role in the Cold War rivalry between the US and the Soviet Union. The NATO consists of 28 Member States, which are mainly European and North American countries. Apart from Turkish and Albanian nationalities, and the Latvian non-citizen status, all NATO nationalities are in the very high quality tier of the QNI.

Most notable movements in the past years are the increased value of the nationalities from Central and Eastern Europe, following their integration in the EU. Albanian nationality also experienced a significant improvement in value of the last five years, which is mainly caused by enhanced Travel Freedom.

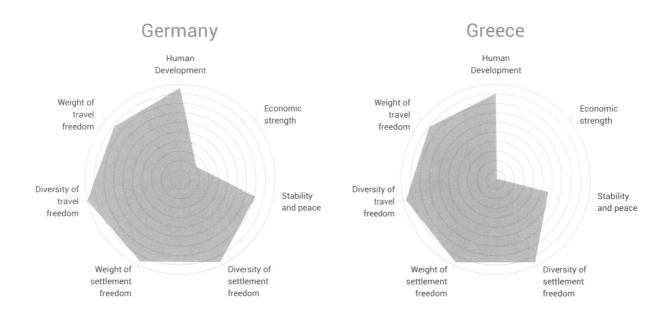

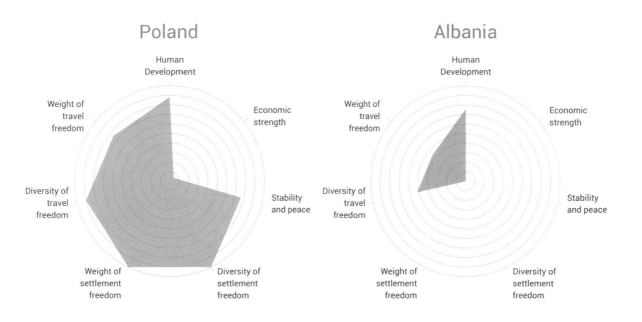

13 Nationalities of microstates

	Nationality	Value 2015	Change in value 2014-2015	Change in value 2011-2015	Overall ranking 2015
1	Liechtenstein	80.0	-0.1	+0.2	12
2	San Marino	48.5	-0.8	+0.1	39
3	Monaco	48.4	-0.6	-0.9	40
4	Andorra	47.0	-1.1	-0.3	42
5	Seychelles	38.3	+0.6	+6.0	56
6	Antigua and Barbuda	38.0	-1.4	-0.6	58
7	St. Kitts and Nevis	37.7	-1.5	-0.3	59
8	St. Lucia	30.3	-1.3	-0.5	86
9	St. Vincent and the Grenadines	29.9	-1.6	-0.9	90
10	Grenada	29.8	-0.6	0.0	91
11	Dominica	29.3	-1.3	+3.6	93
12	Sao Tome and Principe	21.6	0.0	+0.7	133

Mean: 39.90
Median: 37.85

Microstates are fully sovereign states with a very small population or territory. Although various territory-based, population-based or qualitative criteria are available, the QNI defines microstates as states having a population of fewer than 250,000 inhabitants.

The quality of microstate nationalities is generally below average, with a mean of 39.90 (global mean: 38.70) and a median of 37.85 (global mean: 30.90). The notable exceptions are the four European microstates, Liechtenstein, San Marino, Monaco and Andorra. Liechtenstein in particular outperforms the other nationalities as a result of its full integration in the European Economic Area, entailing tremendous Settlement Freedom for its passport holders.

A few notable trends in the quality of microstate nationalities are visible. Passport holders of the Seychelles experienced a substantial quality increase over the last five years. This increase was largely caused by enhanced Travel Freedom: visa-free or visa on arrival travel access was available to 65 destinations in 2011 and 126 destinations in 2015. A similar upward trend can be seen for the nationality of Dominica, of which Travel Freedom Diversity increased from 35 destinations in 2011 to 87 in 2015.

Liechtenstein   Sao Tome and Principe

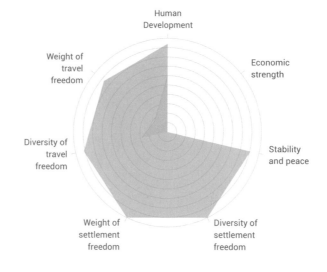

Human Development

Economic strength

Stability and peace

Diversity of settlement freedom

Weight of settlement freedom

Diversity of travel freedom

Weight of travel freedom

San Marino   Grenada

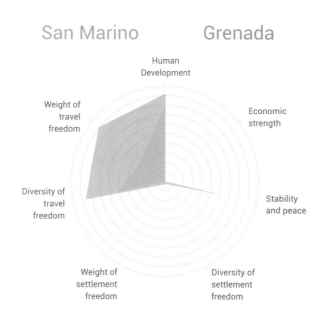

Human Development

Economic strength

Stability and peace

Diversity of settlement freedom

Weight of settlement freedom

Diversity of travel freedom

Weight of travel freedom

C — THE EXTERNAL VALUE OF NATIONALITIES

14 External Value Ranking

	Nationality	Value 2015	Change in value 2014-2015	Change in value 2011-2015
1	Finland	98.4	-0.4	+1.3
2	Sweden	97.6	-0.4	+1.0
3	Denmark	97.4	-0.4	+0.6
4	Norway	96.9	+1.1	+1.2
4	Ireland	96.9	-0.4	+1.1
4	France	96.9	-0.3	-0.2
5	Luxembourg	96.1	-0.9	-1.0
6	Iceland	95.8	+1.0	+1.9
7	Portugal	95.6	-0.3	+0.1
8	Belgium	95.5	-0.5	-0.4
8	UK	95.5	-0.5	-1.1
9	Netherlands	95.4	-0.5	-0.6
9	Germany	95.4	-0.3	-0.1
10	Spain	95.3	-0.3	-0.4
10	Austria	95.3	-0.1	-0.2
10	Italy	95.3	-0.4	-0.5
11	Switzerland	95.1	-0.3	+0.1
12	Greece	95.0	-0.2	+3.4
13	Hungary	94.9	+0.5	+11.3
14	Czech Republic	94.8	+1.4	+11.3
15	Slovakia	94.7	+0.9	+10.4
16	Liechtenstein	94.6	-0.4	-0.1
17	Slovenia	94.4	+0.7	+7.9
18	Latvia	93.9	+0.8	+11.1
19	Malta	93.8	-0.4	+4.3
20	Estonia	93.7	+0.6	+10.7
20	Lithuania	93.7	+0.9	+10.3
21	Poland	91.5	+0.5	+7.0
22	Cyprus	90.0	+1.0	+1.6
23	Bulgaria	87.8	+16.2	+22.8
24	Romania	87.5	+15.8	+21.8
25	Croatia	63.3	+4.2	+28.7
26	Chile	52.9	+3.9	+6.2
27	Argentina	50.9	+0.6	+3.8
28	Singapore	49.4	-1.2	+0.4

	Nationality	Value 2015	Change in value 2014-2015	Change in value 2011-2015
29	New Zealand	49.1	-1.6	+0.4
30	Japan	49.0	-1.7	-1.1
31	Brazil	48.5	-0.4	+3.3
32	Korea (Republic of)	48.2	+0.2	+4.2
33	US	47.5	-1.7	-0.7
33	Australia	47.5	-1.9	-1.6
34	Canada	46.9	-1.5	-0.8
35	Uruguay	46.8	+0.1	+3.6
36	San Marino	46.2	-1.4	-0.1
37	Andorra	44.8	-2.3	-0.4
38	Monaco	44.7	-1.6	-1.1
39	Paraguay	43.7	0.0	+2.6
40	Malaysia	43.4	-1.4	-0.7
41	Brunei Darussalam	42.6	-1.7	-0.9
42	Hong Kong. China (SAR)	41.1	-0.3	+0.4
43	Bahamas	40.8	+1.7	+2.6
44	Israel	39.0	-1.3	-0.9
45	Barbados	36.7	-1.7	-1.4
46	Taiwan	36.5	-0.1	+21.5
47	Venezuela	36.1	0.0	+1.3
48	Mexico	35.3	-1.6	-0.1
49	Mauritius	34.5	+0.6	+2.3
50	Seychelles	34.4	+0.4	+9.2
51	Costa Rica	34.1	-0.8	-0.7
52	St. Kitts and Nevis	33.9	-1.8	-0.4
53	Antigua and Barbuda	33.7	-1.7	-0.8
54	Macao	33.3	+0.5	+3.8
55	Panama	33.0	-1.0	+2.0
56	Peru	32.0	+0.5	+3.6
57	Honduras	31.2	-1.2	-0.6
58	Russian Federation	31.1	+1.2	+5.4
58	Guatemala	31.1	-1.8	-1.1
59	El Salvador	30.4	-2.6	-2.0
59	Gambia	30.4	+0.6	+0.4
60	Serbia	29.6	-0.8	+2.5
61	Sierra Leone	29.2	+0.6	-7.2
62	Benin	29.1	+0.7	+1.0
63	Cape Verde	28.9	+0.1	+2.1
64	Bolivia	28.8	+0.4	+3.9

	Nationality	Value 2015	Change in value 2014-2015	Change in value 2011-2015
64	Nicaragua	28.8	-0.1	+0.6
65	Ecuador	28.7	+8.5	+10.2
66	Ghana	28.5	+0.7	+0.3
67	Macedonia	28.4	+0.1	+2.1
68	Senegal	27.5	+0.5	+1.6
69	Côte d'Ivoire	27.2	+0.4	+1.1
69	United Arab Emirates	27.2	0.0	+1.5
70	Guinea	27.1	+0.3	+0.6
71	Kuwait	27.0	-1.5	-0.4
71	Moldova	27.0	+6.6	+6.8
71	Burkina Faso	27.0	+0.6	+1.0
72	Mali	26.9	+0.3	+0.6
73	Niger	26.8	+0.2	+0.7
74	Qatar	26.7	-0.4	+0.5
74	Togo	26.7	+0.3	+0.8
75	Montenegro	26.5	-1.5	0.0
76	Colombia	26.0	+0.5	+10.6
76	Turkey	26.0	+1.3	+2.1
77	Bosnia and Herzegovina	25.8	-0.4	+10.7
78	Guinea-Bissau	25.7	+0.4	+0.4
78	Liberia	25.7	+0.7	+0.8
79	Nigeria	25.1	+0.4	-0.4
80	Bahrain	24.9	-1.7	-1.5
81	Trinidad and Tobago	24.8	-1.2	-0.3
82	Oman	24.6	-0.5	-0.4
83	Albania	24.2	-0.9	+10.4
84	Saudi Arabia	23.8	-1.4	0.0
85	South Africa	23.4	-1.1	-0.5
86	Ukraine	22.7	-2.6	+1.1
86	Belarus	22.7	-1.2	+1.3
87	St. Lucia	22.4	-1.6	-0.7
88	Kazakhstan	22.2	+1.1	+4.2
89	St. Vincent and the Grenadines	21.7	-1.9	-1.3
90	Belize	21.0	-1.3	-1.0
91	Grenada	20.9	-0.2	+0.2
92	Guyana	20.8	+0.5	+2.8
93	Dominica	20.7	-1.5	+6.2
94	Maldives	20.0	-0.1	+0.4
95	Suriname	19.7	-0.2	+1.3

	Nationality	Value 2015	Change in value 2014-2015	Change in value 2011-2015
96	Jamaica	19.2	0.1	+0.5
97	Thailand	18.1	-1.5	+0.9
98	Papua New Guinea	17.8	+0.1	+0.9
99	Georgia	17.5	+0.3	+1.0
100	Lesotho	17.3	+0.6	+0.8
101	Azerbaijan	16.9	-2.8	-0.4
102	Botswana	16.6	-1.3	-1.6
103	Namibia	16.4	+0.2	-0.3
104	Swaziland	16.1	+0.6	+0.3
104	Tunisia	16.1	+0.1	-0.2
105	Uzbekistan	15.9	-2.8	-1.8
106	Kenya	15.7	+0.3	+0.7
107	Malawi	15.6	+0.0	+0.3
107	Tajikistan	15.6	-2.5	-2.8
108	Philippines	15.5	+0.6	+1.9
109	Kyrgyzstan	15.4	-2.9	-2.4
110	Zambia	15.0	-0.2	0.0
111	Tanzania	14.7	-0.2	+0.7
112	Armenia	14.6	-3.4	-2.6
113	Uganda	14.2	-0.1	+0.6
113	Cuba	14.2	-1.8	+0.7
114	Indonesia	13.9	+0.3	+2.5
115	Zimbabwe	13.7	-0.3	-0.3
116	Dominican Republic	13.4	-1.4	-6.2
117	Morocco	13.3	+0.8	+0.3
118	India	13.0	-0.2	0.0
119	Bhutan	12.5	+0.1	+1.1
120	Cambodia	12.4	+0.3	+2.9
121	Mauritania	12.3	-0.3	+0.2
122	Mongolia	12.0	-0.3	+0.5
123	Laos	11.9	+0.1	+1.6
124	Haiti	11.8	+0.5	+1.0
124	Timor-Leste	11.8	+0.2	+1.4
125	Sao Tome and Principe	11.7	-0.1	+1.1
126	Vietnam	11.6	+0.2	+1.2
127	Mozambique	11.3	+0.1	+0.9
128	(Non-citizen) Latvia	11.2	-0.2	+0.3
128	Turkmenistan	11.2	-1.0	-0.1
129	Egypt	11.0	0.0	+0.9

	Nationality	Value 2015	Change in value 2014-2015	Change in value 2011-2015
129	Madagascar	11.0	-0.4	+0.7
130	Nepal	10.7	-0.3	-0.6
131	Central African Republic	10.6	-0.6	-1.2
131	Gabon	10.6	-0.4	+0.7
132	Algeria	10.5	-0.5	-0.8
132	Chad	10.5	-0.1	+0.8
133	Jordan	10.3	-0.2	+0.9
133	Rwanda	10.3	+0.1	+1.2
134	China	10.2	+0.2	+1.3
135	Myanmar	10.1	+0.2	+2.2
135	Cameroon	10.1	+0.1	+0.5
136	Yemen	9.9	-0.3	+0.7
137	Comoros	9.8	-0.3	+1.1
138	Congo (Democratic Republic of the)	9.7	-0.3	+0.1
139	Equatorial Guinea	9.5	-0.2	+0.9
140	Djibouti	9.4	+0.1	-1.1
141	Angola	9.3	+0.1	+1.4
142	Burundi	9.2	-0.2	+0.7
143	Iran	9.0	-0.5	+0.8
143	Kosovo	9.0	+0.2	+0.1
143	Lebanon	9.0	-1.5	0.0
144	Bangladesh	8.9	0.0	-0.5
145	Libya	8.7	-0.5	-0.8
145	Congo	8.7	-0.1	+0.4
145	Ethiopia	8.7	-0.7	+0.9
146	Sri Lanka	8.5	+0.2	-1.2
147	Eritrea	8.3	+0.1	+0.7
147	Sudan	8.3	-0.5	+1.5
148	Palestinian Territory	7.9	-0.5	0.0
148	Syria	7.9	-1.2	-1.3
149	Iraq	6.9	-1.7	-0.7
150	Pakistan	6.7	-0.3	-1.3
151	Afghanistan	6.0	-0.2	+0.2

15 Risers and fallers in 2015

Top 5 risers

	Nationality	Change in value	Change in ranking
1	Bulgaria	+16.2	+3
2	Romania	+15.8	+1
3	Ecuador	+8.5	+32
4	Moldova	+6.6	+23
5	Croatia	+4.1	+2

Top 5 fallers

	Nationality	Change in value	Change in ranking
1	Armenia	-3.4	-7
2	Kyrgyzstan	-2.9	-6
3	Uzbekistan	-2.8	-3
4	Azerbaijan	-2.7	-2
5	El Salvador	-2.6	-3
5	Ukraine	-2.6	-3

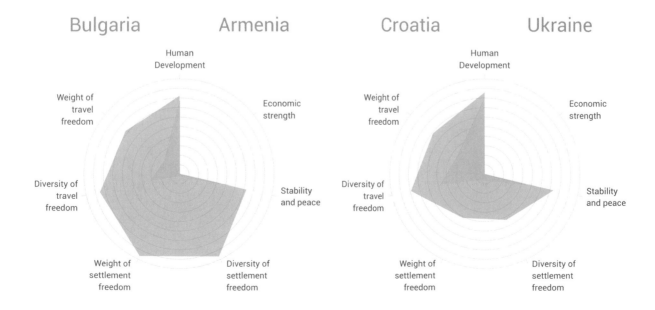

16 Risers and fallers in 2011–2015

Top 5 risers

	Nationality	Change in value	Change in ranking
1	Croatia	+28.7	+22
2	Bulgaria	+22.8	0
2	Romania	+22.8	-2
4	Taiwan	+21.5	+59
5	Czech Republic	+11.3	+3

Top 5 fallers

	Nationality	Change in value	Change in ranking
1	Sierra Leone	-7.3	-17
2	Dominican Republic	-6.2	-30
3	Tajikistan	-2.8	-18
4	Armenia	-2.6	-16
5	Kyrgyzstan	-2.4	-16

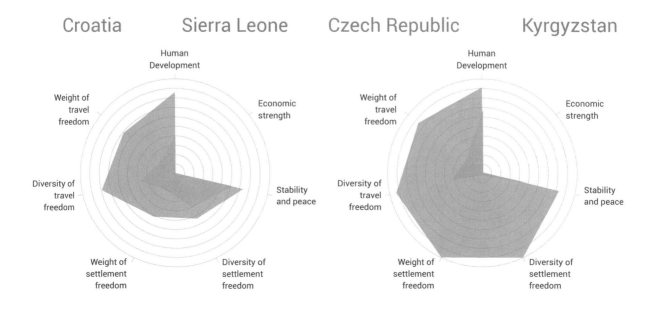

Croatia Sierra Leone Czech Republic Kyrgyzstan

17 Regional trends in the External Value of Nationalities

Regional trends in external value 2014–2015

	Nationality	Change in value	Change in ranking
1	South America	+1.19	+22
2	Europe	+0.57	0
3	Sub-Saharan Africa	+0.07	-2
4	Asia and the Pacific	-0,52	+59
5	Middle East and North Africa	-0.57	+3
6	Central America and the Caribbean	-1.09	+59
7	North America	-1.58	+3

Regional trends in external value 2011–2015

	Nationality	Change in value	Change in ranking
1	South America	+4.44	+22
2	Europe	+4.20	0
3	Asia and the Pacific	+1.15	-2
4	Sub-Saharan Africa	+0.56	+59
5	Middle East and North Africa	+0.09	+3
6	Central America and the Caribbean	-0.14	+59
7	North America	-0.78	+3

D — THE SETTLEMENT FREEDOM OF NATIONALITIES

18 Settlement Freedom Ranking

	Nationality	Value 2015	Change in value 2014-2015	Change in value 2011-2015
1	Slovakia	100.0	0.0	+13.3
1	Latvia	100.0	0.0	+13.3
1	Liechtenstein	100.0	0.0	0.0
1	Hungary	100.0	0.0	+13.3
2	Lithuania	99.9	0.0	+13.2
2	Estonia	99.9	0.0	+13.2
2	Slovenia	99.9	0.0	+13.3
2	Czech Republic	99.9	0.0	+13.2
2	Poland	99.9	0.0	+13.3
3	Finland	99.8	0.0	+3.0
3	Iceland	99.8	+3.0	+3.0
3	France	99.8	0.0	+0.0
3	Ireland	99.8	0.0	+3.1
3	Denmark	99.8	0.0	+3.1
3	Sweden	99.8	0.0	+3.1
4	Norway	99.7	+3.1	+3.0
5	Malta	96.8	-0.1	-0.1
5	Portugal	96.8	-0.1	-0.1
6	Cyprus	96.7	-0.1	-0.2
6	Greece	96.7	-0.1	-0.1
6	Luxembourg	96.7	-0.1	-0.1
7	Austria	96.6	-0.1	-0.2
7	Belgium	96.6	-0.1	-0.2
7	Switzerland	96.6	-0.1	-0.1
8	Spain	96.5	-0.1	-0.2
8	Netherlands	96.5	-0.1	-0.2
8	Bulgaria	96.5	+29.4	+42.8
8	Romania	96.5	+29.5	+42.8
8	Italy	96.5	-0.1	-0.1
9	UK	96.4	-0.1	-0.1
10	Germany	96.2	-0.2	-0.2
11	Croatia	52.3	+5.2	+52.3
12	Benin	32.2	+1.0	+1.2
12	Cape Verde	32.2	+1.0	+1.2
13	Niger	29.9	+0.9	+1.1

	Nationality	Value 2015	Change in value 2014-2015	Change in value 2011-2015
13	Sierra Leone	29.9	+1.0	+1.2
14	Burkina Faso	29.8	+0.9	+1.1
14	Guinea	29.8	+0.9	+1.1
14	Guinea-Bissau	29.8	+0.9	+1.2
14	Mali	29.8	+0.9	+1.2
14	Liberia	29.8	+0.9	+1.1
15	Gambia	29.7	+0.9	+1.1
15	Côte d'Ivoire	29.7	+0.9	+1.1
15	Togo	29.7	+0.9	+1.2
15	Senegal	29.7	+1.0	+1.2
16	Nigeria	29.5	+0.9	+1.1
16	Ghana	29.5	+0.9	+1.1
17	Paraguay	22.3	+1.0	+4.0
18	Bolivia	21.9	+0.6	+3.6
19	Uruguay	21.7	+0.6	+3.6
20	Chile	21.6	+0.6	+3.6
20	Argentina	21.6	+0.6	+3.6
21	Peru	21.5	+0.2	+3.2
22	Brazil	20.4	0.0	+2.6
23	Ecuador	18.6	+15.6	+15.7
24	Colombia	18.3	+0.2	+15.4
25	Oman	16.2	-2.5	-2.4
26	Bahrain	16.1	-2.5	-2.4
26	Kuwait	16.1	-2.5	-2.4
26	United Arab Emirates	16.1	-2.4	-2.4
27	Qatar	16.0	-2.5	-2.4
27	Saudi Arabia	16.0	-2.5	-2.4
28	Belarus	15.4	-2.5	+0.6
29	Kazakhstan	12.4	+0.4	+3.5
30	Russian Federation	12.1	+0.4	+3.4
31	Andorra	7.0	-2.8	-2.8
32	Azerbaijan	6.0	-6.1	-2.9
33	Moldova	5.9	-6.0	-6.0
33	Georgia	5.9	+0.2	+0.3
33	Tajikistan	5.9	-6.0	-6.0
33	Ukraine	5.9	-5.3	-5.1
33	Uzbekistan	5.9	-6.0	-6.0
34	US	5.1	-2.8	-2.8
35	Monaco	3.6	-2.8	-2.8

	Nationality	Value 2015	Change in value 2014-2015	Change in value 2011-2015
36	New Zealand	3.5	-2.9	+0.3
36	San Marino	3.5	-2.9	-2.9
36	Nepal	3.5	+0.2	+0.3
37	Australia	3.4	-2.8	-2.8
38	Guyana	3.3	+0.1	+3.3
38	Suriname	3.3	+0.1	+0.4
38	Venezuela	3.3	+0.1	+0.2
39	Kyrgyzstan	3.0	-6.2	-6.1
40	Armenia	2.8	-6.2	-6.1
41	India	2.7	+0.1	+0.1
42	(Non-citizen) Latvia	0.0	0.0	0.0
42	Cuba	0.0	-3.0	-2.9
42	Dominica	0.0	-3.0	-2.9
42	Maldives	0.0	0.0	-1.6
42	Canada	0.0	-3.0	-2.9
42	Japan	0.0	-3.0	-2.9
42	Afghanistan	0.0	0.0	0.0
42	Albania	0.0	-3.0	-2.9
42	Algeria	0.0	0.0	0.0
42	Angola	0.0	0.0	0.0
42	Antigua and Barbuda	0.0	-3.0	-2.9
42	Bahamas	0.0	0.0	0.0
42	Bangladesh	0.0	0.0	0.0
42	Barbados	0.0	-3.0	-2.9
42	Belize	0.0	-3.0	-3.6
42	Bhutan	0.0	0.0	0.0
42	Bosnia and Herzegovina	0.0	-3.0	-2.9
42	Botswana	0.0	-3.0	-2.9
42	Brunei Darussalam	0.0	-3.0	-2.9
42	Burundi	0.0	0.0	0.0
42	Cambodia	0.0	0.0	0.0
42	Cameroon	0.0	0.0	0.0
42	Central African Republic	0.0	0.0	0.0
42	Chad	0.0	0.0	0.0
42	China	0.0	0.0	0.0
42	Taiwan	0.0	0.0	0.0
42	Comoros	0.0	0.0	0.0
42	Congo	0.0	0.0	0.0
42	Congo (Democratic Republic of the)	0.0	0.0	0.0

	Nationality	Value 2015	Change in value 2014-2015	Change in value 2011-2015
42	Costa Rica	0.0	-3.0	-2.9
42	Djibouti	0.0	0.0	0.0
42	Dominican Republic	0.0	-3.0	-2.9
42	Egypt	0.0	0.0	0.0
42	El Salvador	0.0	-3.0	-2.9
42	Equatorial Guinea	0.0	0.0	0.0
42	Eritrea	0.0	0.0	0.0
42	Ethiopia	0.0	0.0	0.0
42	Gabon	0.0	0.0	0.0
42	Grenada	0.0	0.0	0.0
42	Guatemala	0.0	-3.0	-2.9
42	Haiti	0.0	0.0	0.0
42	Honduras	0.0	-3.0	-2.9
42	Hong Kong. China (SAR)	0.0	0.0	0.0
42	Indonesia	0.0	0.0	0.0
42	Iran	0.0	0.0	0.0
42	Iraq	0.0	-3.0	-2.9
42	Israel	0.0	-3.0	-3.6
42	Jamaica	0.0	0.0	0.0
42	Jordan	0.0	0.0	0.0
42	Kenya	0.0	0.0	0.0
42	Korea (Republic of)	0.0	-3.0	-2.9
42	Kosovo	0.0	0.0	0.0
42	Laos	0.0	0.0	0.0
42	Lebanon	0.0	-3.0	-2.9
42	Lesotho	0.0	0.0	0.0
42	Libya	0.0	0.0	0.0
42	Macedonia	0.0	0.0	0.0
42	Macao	0.0	0.0	0.0
42	Madagascar	0.0	0.0	0.0
42	Malawi	0.0	0.0	0.0
42	Malaysia	0.0	-3.0	-3.6
42	Mauritania	0.0	0.0	0.0
42	Mauritius	0.0	-3.0	-1.3
42	Mexico	0.0	-3.0	-2.9
42	Mongolia	0.0	0.0	0.0
42	Montenegro	0.0	-3.0	-2.9
42	Morocco	0.0	0.0	0.0
42	Mozambique	0.0	0.0	0.0

	Nationality	Value 2015	Change in value 2014-2015	Change in value 2011-2015
42	Myanmar	0.0	0.0	0.0
42	Namibia	0.0	0.0	0.0
42	Nicaragua	0.0	0.0	0.0
42	Pakistan	0.0	0.0	0.0
42	Palestinian Territory	0.0	0.0	0.0
42	Panama	0.0	-3.0	-1.3
42	Papua New Guinea	0.0	0.0	0.0
42	Philippines	0.0	0.0	0.0
42	Rwanda	0.0	0.0	0.0
42	St. Kitts and Nevis	0.0	-3.0	-1.3
42	St. Lucia	0.0	-3.0	-1.3
42	St. Vincent and the Grenadines	0.0	-3.0	-1.3
42	Sao Tome and Principe	0.0	0.0	0.0
42	Serbia	0.0	-3.0	-2.9
42	Seychelles	0.0	-3.0	-2.9
42	Singapore	0.0	-3.0	-1.3
42	South Africa	0.0	-3.0	-2.9
42	Sri Lanka	0.0	0.0	0.0
42	Sudan	0.0	0.0	0.0
42	Swaziland	0.0	0.0	0.0
42	Syria	0.0	0.0	0.0
42	Tanzania	0.0	0.0	0.0
42	Thailand	0.0	-3.0	-2.9
42	Timor-Leste	0.0	0.0	0.0
42	Trinidad and Tobago	0.0	-3.0	-2.9
42	Tunisia	0.0	0.0	0.0
42	Turkey	0.0	0.0	0.0
42	Turkmenistan	0.0	-3.0	-2.9
42	Uganda	0.0	0.0	0.0
42	Vietnam	0.0	0.0	0.0
42	Yemen	0.0	0.0	0.0
42	Zambia	0.0	0.0	0.0
42	Zimbabwe	0.0	0.0	0.0

19 Risers and fallers in 2015

Top 5 risers

	Nationality	Change in value	Change in ranking
1	Romania	+29.5	+3
2	Bulgaria	+29.4	+2
3	Ecuador	+15.6	+19
4	Croatia	+5.2	+1
5	Iceland	+3.1	+3

Top 5 fallers

	Nationality	Change in value	Change in ranking
1	Armenia	-6.2	-5
1	Kyrgyzstan	-6.2	-5
3	Azerbaijan	-6.1	-4
3	Moldova	-6.1	-3
3	Tajikistan	-6.1	-3
3	Uzbekistan	-6.1	-3

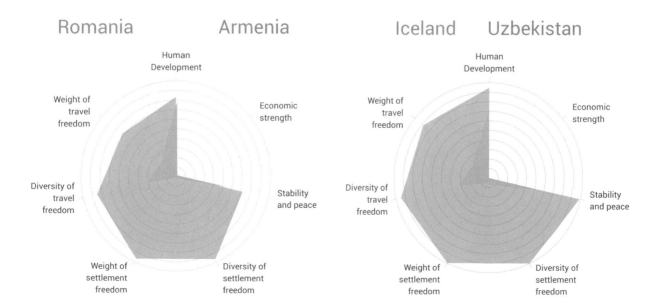

Romania   Armenia

Iceland   Uzbekistan

20 Risers and fallers in 2011–2015

Top 5 risers

	Nationality	Change in value	Change in ranking
1	Croatia	+52.3	+36
2	Romania	+42.8	+6
2	Bulgaria	+42.8	+6
3	Ecuador	+15.6	+20
4	Colombia	+15.3	+19

Top 5 fallers

	Nationality	Change in value	Change in ranking
1	Kyrgyzstan	-6.1	-7
1	Armenia	-6.1	-7
2	Uzbekistan	-6.0	-4
2	Tajikistan	-6.0	-4
2	Moldova	-6.0	-4

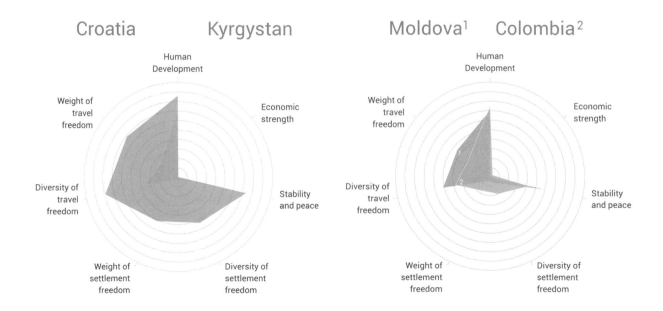

21 Regional trends in the Settlement Freedom of Nationalities

Regional trends in Settlement Freedom 2014–2015

	Nationality	Change in value	Change in ranking
1	South America	+1.63	+22
2	Europe	+0.47	0
3	Sub-Saharan Africa	+0.04	-2
4	Middle East and North Africa	-1.13	+59
5	Asia and the Pacific	-1.30	+3
6	Central America and the Caribbean	-2.25	+59
7	North America	-2.88	+3

Regional trends in Settlement Freedom 2011–2015

	Nationality	Change in value	Change in ranking
1	South America	+4.91	+22
2	Europe	+4.58	0
3	Sub-Saharan Africa	+0.16	-2
4	Asia and the Pacific	-1.12	+59
5	Middle East and North Africa	-1.14	+3
6	Central America and the Caribbean	-1.97	+59
7	North America	-2.86	+3

E – THE TRAVEL FREEDOM OF NATIONALITIES

22 Travel Freedom Ranking

	Nationality	Value 2015	Change in value 2014–2015	Change in value 2011–2015
1	Singapore	98.9	+0.6	+2.2
2	Japan	98.1	-0.3	+0.8
3	Finland	96.9	-0.9	-0.6
4	Korea (Republic of)	96.4	+3.3	+11.4
5	Luxembourg	95.6	-1.7	-1.8
6	Sweden	95.4	-0.9	-1.0
7	Denmark	95.0	-0.9	-1.9
8	New Zealand	94.8	-0.3	+0.6
9	UK	94.6	-0.8	-2.0
10	Portugal	94.5	-0.4	+0.4
10	Germany	94.5	-0.5	0.0
11	Belgium	94.4	-0.9	-0.6
12	Netherlands	94.3	-0.9	-1.0
13	Spain	94.1	-0.5	-0.6
13	Norway	94.1	-0.9	-0.6
14	Austria	94.0	-0.1	-0.2
14	Italy	94.0	-0.9	-0.9
14	Ireland	94.0	-0.9	-0.9
15	France	93.9	-0.7	-0.4
16	Canada	93.8	-0.1	+1.3
17	Switzerland	93.6	-0.5	+0.2
18	Greece	93.3	-0.4	+6.9
19	Iceland	91.7	-1.2	+0.7
20	Australia	91.5	-1.0	-0.6
21	Malta	90.9	-0.6	+8.8
22	US	90.0	-0.4	+1.4
23	Hungary	89.9	+1.0	+9.4
24	Czech Republic	89.7	+2.8	+9.4
25	Slovakia	89.5	+1.8	+7.6
26	Liechtenstein	89.2	-0.8	-0.1
27	San Marino	88.9	0.0	+2.7
28	Slovenia	88.8	+1.3	+2.4
29	Latvia	87.9	+1.7	+9.1
30	Estonia	87.5	+1.3	+8.2
31	Lithuania	87.4	+1.7	+7.4

	Nationality	Value 2015	Change in value 2014-2015	Change in value 2011-2015
32	Malaysia	86.9	+0.4	+2.3
33	Monaco	85.9	-0.4	+0.8
34	Brunei Darussalam	85.3	-0.3	+1.3
35	Chile	84.1	+7.1	+8.8
36	Cyprus	83.2	+2.0	+3.3
37	Poland	83.1	+0.9	+0.7
38	Andorra	82.6	-1.8	+1.9
39	Hong Kong. China (SAR)	82.1	-0.6	+0.8
40	Bahamas	81.6	+3.4	+5.2
41	Argentina	80.2	+0.6	+3.9
42	Bulgaria	79.2	+3.0	+2.9
43	Romania	78.6	+2.1	+0.8
44	Israel	78.0	+0.3	+1.7
45	Brazil	76.5	-1.0	+4.0
46	Croatia	74.2	+3.1	+5.0
47	Barbados	73.5	-0.4	+0.2
48	Taiwan	73.0	-0.1	+43.1
49	Uruguay	71.8	-0.4	+3.5
50	Mexico	70.6	-0.2	+2.8
51	Mauritius	69.1	+4.3	+6.1
52	Venezuela	69.0	0.0	+2.6
53	Seychelles	68.9	+3.9	+21.4
54	Costa Rica	68.2	+1.4	+1.6
55	St. Kitts and Nevis	67.8	-0.6	+0.5
56	Antigua and Barbuda	67.4	-0.4	+1.3
57	Macao	66.6	+1.1	+7.6
58	Panama	66.1	+1.0	+5.4
59	Paraguay	65.2	-0.8	+1.3
60	Honduras	62.3	+0.5	+1.7
60	Guatemala	62.3	-0.5	+0.8
61	El Salvador	60.8	-2.3	-1.1
62	Serbia	59.2	+1.4	+7.9
63	Nicaragua	57.6	-0.1	+1.1
64	Macedonia	56.8	+0.2	+4.3
65	Montenegro	53.0	-0.1	+2.9
66	Turkey	51.9	+2.4	+4.2
67	Bosnia and Herzegovina	51.6	+2.2	+24.3
68	Russian Federation	50.2	+2.2	+7.5
69	Trinidad and Tobago	49.5	+0.5	+2.3

	Nationality	Value 2015	Change in value 2014-2015	Change in value 2011-2015
70	Albania	48.3	+1.0	+23.6
71	Moldova	48.1	+19.2	-9.3
72	South Africa	46.9	+0.8	+2.1
73	St. Lucia	44.9	-0.2	0.0
74	St. Vincent and the Grenadines	43.3	-0.9	-1.4
75	Peru	42.5	+0.8	+4.0
76	Belize	41.9	+0.2	+1.4
77	Grenada	41.8	-0.3	+0.5
78	Dominica	41.4	-0.1	+15.3
79	Maldives	39.9	-0.4	+2.2
80	Ukraine	39.6	+0.1	+7.4
81	Ecuador	38.9	+1.4	+4.9
82	Jamaica	38.5	+0.2	+1.1
83	Guyana	38.3	+0.8	+2.3
84	United Arab Emirates	38.2	+2.3	+5.3
85	Kuwait	37.9	-0.5	+1.6
86	Qatar	37.3	+1.6	+3.3
87	Suriname	36.2	-0.5	+2.4
88	Thailand	36.1	-0.1	+4.6
89	Bolivia	35.7	+0.2	+4.1
89	Papua New Guinea	35.7	+0.4	+1.9
90	Lesotho	34.5	+1.1	+1.5
91	Colombia	33.8	+0.8	+5.9
92	Bahrain	33.7	-0.8	-0.6
93	Botswana	33.2	+0.4	-0.3
94	Oman	33.0	+1.4	+1.6
95	Namibia	32.8	+0.4	-0.5
96	Swaziland	32.2	+1.2	+0.7
97	Tunisia	32.1	0.0	-0.5
97	Kazakhstan	32.1	+1.9	+5.0
98	Saudi Arabia	31.6	-0.2	+2.4
99	Kenya	31.3	+0.6	+1.3
99	Malawi	31.3	+0.1	+0.7
100	Gambia	31.1	+0.2	-0.3
101	Philippines	31.0	+1.1	+3.9
102	Zambia	30.0	-0.3	0.0
102	Belarus	30.0	+0.1	+2.0
103	Tanzania	29.4	-0.4	+1.3
104	Georgia	29.2	+0.4	+1.8

	Nationality	Value 2015	Change in value 2014-2015	Change in value 2011-2015
105	Sierra Leone	28.5	+0.3	-15.6
106	Uganda	28.4	-0.2	+1.1
107	Cuba	28.3	-0.7	+4.3
108	Azerbaijan	27.9	+0.6	+2.3
109	Indonesia	27.7	+0.5	+5.0
109	Kyrgyzstan	27.7	+0.4	+1.2
110	Ghana	27.4	+0.3	-0.7
110	Zimbabwe	27.4	-0.5	-0.6
111	Dominican Republic	26.8	+0.1	-9.5
112	Morocco	26.7	+1.7	+0.8
113	Armenia	26.4	-0.6	+1.0
114	Benin	25.9	+0.4	+0.7
114	Uzbekistan	25.9	+0.4	+2.3
115	Cape Verde	25.6	-0.8	+3.0
116	Tajikistan	25.3	+1.0	+0.3
116	Senegal	25.3	+0.1	+1.9
117	Bhutan	24.9	0.0	+2.1
117	Cambodia	24.9	+0.6	+6.0
118	Côte d'Ivoire	24.6	-0.3	+1.0
119	Mauritania	24.5	-0.8	+0.4
120	Guinea	24.4	-0.3	0.0
121	Burkina Faso	24.1	+0.1	+0.9
121	Mongolia	24.1	-0.6	+1.2
122	Mali	24.0	-0.4	0.0
123	Niger	23.8	-0.3	+0.5
123	Laos	23.8	+0.2	+3.1
124	Togo	23.7	-0.3	+0.5
124	Haiti	23.7	+1.1	+2.1
125	Timor-Leste	23.6	+0.5	+2.9
126	Sao Tome and Principe	23.4	-0.3	+2.2
127	India	23.3	-0.5	-0.1
128	Vietnam	23.2	+0.5	+2.5
129	Mozambique	22.7	+0.2	+1.8
130	Turkmenistan	22.4	+1.0	+2.8
131	(Non-citizen) Latvia	22.3	-0.5	+0.5
132	Egypt	22.1	0.0	+1.8
132	Madagascar	22.1	-0.7	+1.5
133	Liberia	21.5	+0.4	+0.4
133	Guinea-Bissau	21.5	-0.3	-0.5

	Nationality	Value 2015	Change in value 2014-2015	Change in value 2011-2015
134	Central African Republic	21.3	-1.1	-2.3
134	Gabon	21.3	-0.7	+1.5
135	Algeria	20.9	-1.1	-1.8
135	Chad	20.9	-0.3	+1.5
136	Jordan	20.7	-0.3	+1.9
136	Nigeria	20.7	0.0	-1.9
137	Rwanda	20.5	+0.2	+2.3
138	China	20.3	+0.2	+2.5
139	Myanmar	20.2	+0.4	+4.4
139	Cameroon	20.2	+0.3	+0.9
140	Yemen	19.9	-0.4	+1.5
141	Comoros	19.7	-0.4	+2.2
142	Congo	19.3	-0.7	+0.1
143	Equatorial Guinea	19.1	-0.3	+1.8
144	Djibouti	18.8	+0.2	-2.2
145	Angola	18.6	+0.2	+2.9
146	Burundi	18.5	-0.2	+1.4
147	Iran	18.1	-0.9	+1.6
148	Nepal	18.0	-0.7	-1.4
149	Kosovo	17.9	+0.4	+0.1
149	Lebanon	17.9	-0.1	+2.8
149	Bangladesh	17.9	0.0	-0.9
150	Libya	17.5	-0.9	-1.5
151	Congo (Democratic Republic of the)	17.4	-0.3	+0.7
152	Ethiopia	17.3	-1.5	+1.6
153	Sri Lanka	16.9	+0.2	-2.5
154	Eritrea	16.6	+0.3	+1.3
154	Sudan	16.6	-0.9	+2.9
155	Palestinian Territory	15.8	-1.0	0.0
155	Syria	15.8	-2.4	-2.7
156	Iraq	13.8	-0.4	+1.6
157	Pakistan	13.4	-0.6	-2.7
158	Afghanistan	11.9	-0.5	+0.3

23 Risers and fallers in 2015

Top 5 risers

	Nationality	Change in value	Change in ranking
1	Moldova	+19.3	+32
2	Chile	+7.1	+5
3	Mauritius	+4.3	+5
4	Seychelles	+3.9	+2
5	Bahamas	+3.4	-3

Top 5 fallers

	Nationality	Change in value	Change in ranking
1	Syria	-2.5	-2
2	El Salvador	-2.3	-4
3	Andorra	-1.8	-6
4	Luxembourg	-1.7	-1
5	Ethiopia	-1.5	-3

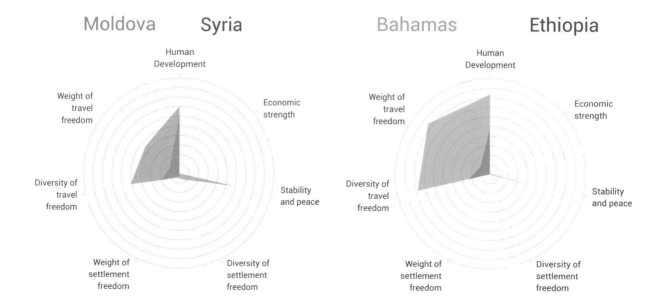

24 Risers and fallers in 2011–2015

Top 5 risers

	Nationality	Change in value	Change in ranking
1	Taiwan	+43.1	+45
2	Bosnia and Herzegovina	+24.3	+32
3	Albania	+23.6	+38
4	Seychelles	+21.4	+12
5	Moldova	+19.7	+23

Top 5 fallers

	Nationality	Change in value	Change in ranking
1	Sierra Leone	-15.7	-36
2	Dominican Republic	-9.5	-35
3	Syria	-2.7	-18
4	Pakistan	-2.6	-11
5	Sri Lanka	-2.5	-22

Sierra Leone[1] Moldova[2] Albania[1] Sri Lanka[2]

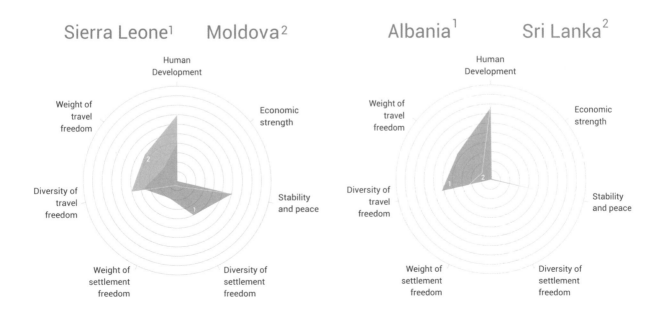

25 Regional trends in the Settlement Freedom of Nationalities

Regional trends in travel freedom 2014–2015

	Nationality	Change in value	Change in ranking
1	South America	+2.23	+22
2	Central America and the Caribbean	+0.32	0
3	Europe	+0.26	-2
4	Asia and the Pacific	+0.26	+59
5	Sub-Sarahan Africa	+0.1	+3
6	Middle East and North Africa	-0.02	+59
7	North America	-0.29	+3

Regional trends in travel freedom 2011–2015

	Nationality	Change in value	Change in ranking
1	South America	+3.96	+22
2	Europe	+3.82	0
3	Asia and the Pacific	+3.42	-2
4	Central America and the Caribbean	+1.69	+59
5	Middle East and North Africa	+1.32	+3
6	North America	+1.31	+59
7	Sub-Saharan Africa	+0.96	+3

Part 3

EXPERT COMMENTARY

United States Citizenship

Peter Spiro
Beasley School of Law,
Temple University

The US presents a study in QNI contrasts. The country is ranked at the top of the QNI index on the Economic Strength element and near the top with respect to Human Development. It has excellent quality with respect to Travel Freedom, reflecting the fact that US passport holders are admitted to an overwhelming majority of states on a visa-free or visa-on-arrival basis. However, it scores very low on the Settlement Freedom element. Those low scores, combined with an anemic showing on Peace and Stability, put the US at a general rank of 28th — a very high quality nationality, but not in the top 25 of the world — a placement that has held relatively steady over the last five years.

The undeniable desirability of a US passport is anchored in two benefits. First, it gives the holder unrestricted home access to the world's most powerful economy. The US is restrictive in allocating permanent residence and business-related non-immigrant admissions. It is difficult as a non-citizen to secure long-term residence in the US even in skilled and professional occupations. The US passport thus represents a major economic resource in terms of enhanced employment opportunities. Relatedly, the US scores high on the Human Development element, which reflects such factors as life expectancy, average age of schooling, and per capita gross national income. Second, the US ranks high in terms of Travel Freedom. US passport holders are admitted visa-free or visa-on-arrival in almost all other states.

The US scores less impressively on the Peace and Stability element. This tracks a middle of the pack ranking in the Global Peace Index. Some input factors to that index reflect the country's superpower status, for instance, the level of its nuclear arsenal and its engagement in external conflicts. It also reflects a higher level of crime and especially incarceration than in other developed states. Most of these factors will not diminish the value of a US passport for the typical holder. Weighing more heavily on the US ranking is the low score on Settlement Freedom. US citizens are entitled to settle long-term in only a small handful of minor economies (only three in 2015, down from four in previous years). As a result, the US ranks behind

all states of the EU and the European Economic Area, which have full reciprocal access to between 29 and 31 countries. This depresses its QNI External Value Ranking, down slightly to 28th place in the 2015 tally.

The rankings for the US have been stable in recent years, and there is no reason to expect major changes in coming years. Travel Freedom will almost certainly continue to rank at or near the top. There is little prospect in the immediate future that US citizens will secure Settlement Freedom in major economies. Despite its middling score in the QNI, US citizenship constitutes a valuable commodity.[20] Holders may wish to diversify their passport portfolio for expanded global long-term employment and residential opportunities.

20 It is important to note that the QNI does not take tax rules into account. On this criterion the US nationality is one of the most atypical in the world, which is also one of the main reasons behind the high number of the renunciations of US citizenship by Americans living abroad and holding other nationalities

Citizenship of the European Union

Dimitry Kochenov LAPA,
Princeton University;
University of Groningen,
The Netherlands

Although the EU is not a state, it boasts a citizenship like many others, established more than 20 years ago by the Treaty of Maastricht. This citizenship allows the Union to distinguish between 'European citizens' and foreigners, called 'third-country nationals' in contemporary Eurospeak. By law, every national of each of the EU's 28 Member States is also a citizen of the Union. EU citizens enjoy an array of important rights, including residence, work and non-discrimination, in the territory of the Union, as well as some political rights, including in European Parliament elections and municipal elections. As the biggest economy in the world and boasting very high levels of human development, the EU can legitimately be expected to be the site of one of the best nationalities in the world — and it is. EU citizenship has steadily occupied one of the leading places among the nationalities of very high quality in the QNI ranking, placed just above US citizenship and thus also above those of Australia, Canada and Japan. Indeed, should the individual EU nationalities be excluded from the QNI index, EU citizenship would then end up in the top five, right under Norway, Iceland, Switzerland and Liechtenstein and just above the US, steadily occupying the 5th or 6th place in the world.

While Europeans travel on standardized EU-model burgundy-colored passports, which display all the information in the 24 official languages of the EU, the majority of foreign countries will not — and are not actually asked to — recognize the existence of EU nationality as such. EU citizenship is a legal construct mostly for the internal consumption within the EU. The only exception from this rule is the right which EU citizens enjoy outside the EU to receive protection and services from the consulates of any EU Member State in the countries where their own Union Member State of nationality is not represented. It goes without saying that this right is of huge importance, in particular, for the EU citizens coming from the small Member States, which cannot boast large networks of diplomatic and consular offices worldwide. The EU citizenship right to receive protection abroad will thus be of much greater importance for a Maltese or Lithuanian EU national, than for a German or a Pole. Since the classical legal

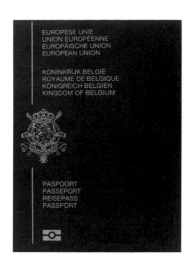

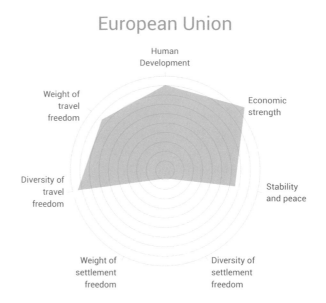

European Union

Human Development

Economic strength

Stability and peace

Diversity of settlement freedom

Weight of settlement freedom

Diversity of travel freedom

Weight of travel freedom

QNI ranking of top ten world's nationalities with all the individual EU Member States excluded

2011	2012	2013	2014	2015
1.Norway 81.5	1.Norway 81.6	1.Norway 80.9 1.Iceland 80.9	1.Norway 81.2	1.Norway 81.7
2.Switzerland 80.7	2.Iceland 81.2	2.Switzerland 80.8	2.Iceland 81.1	2.Iceland 81.6
3.Iceland 80.5	3.Liechtensten 77.5	3.Liechtenstein 79.9	3.Switzerland 81	3.Switzerland 80.7
4.Liechtenstein 79.8	4.Switzerland 77.3	4.EU 67.8	4.Liechtenstein 80.1	4.Liechtenstein 80
5.EU 68.4	5.EU 69.2	5.US 64	5.EU 68.01	5.EU 67.4
6.US 63.9	6.US 63.9	6.Japan 57.2	6.US 64.5	6.US 63.4
7.Japan 57.4	7.Japan 57.5	7.New Zealand 54.6	7.Japan 57.5	7.Japan 56.2
8.New Zealand 53.4	8.Australia 53	8.Australia 53.2	8.New Zealand 54.3	8.New Zealand 53.4
9.Australia 53.1	9.Canada 52.2	9.Canada 52.9	9.Canada 53.6	9.Canada 52.7
10.Canada 52.3	10.Singapore 51.3	10.Singapore 52.8	10.Australia 53.2	10.Australia 52.5

orthodoxy connects nationalities with states recognized as such by the international community, all EU citizens become nationals, uniquely, of their particular states as they travel. This allows foreign countries to treat EU citizens holding the nationalities of different Member States differently. In one example, while the absolute majority of EU citizens can travel to the US visa-free, EU citizens whose Union status derives from the nationalities of Bulgaria, Croatia, Cyprus, Poland, Romania do not enjoy this possibility. To reflect this reality, the QNI looks at the average values of the weight and diversity of travel freedom enjoyed by all the nationalities of the EU to come up with the figure for the nationality of the Union. This explains why EU nationality actually occupies a lower place on the QNI rankings than the nationalities of many of the individual Member States of the Union, such as German, Estonian and Finnish, for instance. The discrepancy between German nationality and the general EU nationality is even better explained by looking at the settlement freedom – since EU nationality works in all of the EU territory, the internal ability to settle across EU Member States which is enjoyed by EU nationals is not taken into account as an external component of the quality of EU nationality. This is only logical, since when QNI ranks nationalities of federations, like Brazil, Russia, or the US, the ability to travel between individual states within the federations is not taken into account outside of the scope of the factors contributing to the internal quality of the given nationality. The EU is no different for the purposes of the QNI methodology. This explains even better the fact that the quality of EU nationality is lower than that of some of the EU's component parts – the Member States. German nationality, to return to the same example, benefits form the added external value of the settlement rights which all the Germans enjoy in other Member States of the EU, while EU nationality only boasts settlement rights in some countries outside of the Union, like Iceland, Norway and Switzerland.

All in all, the QNI makes it absolutely clear that the quality of EU and US nationalities has consistently remained at a relatively similar, very high level. Importantly, while being attached to extremely important economies, both nationalities enjoy a high level of preferential treatment around the world through asymmetrical travel access for short term tourist and business travel: just like Americans, Europeans are not required to obtain visas in advance to visit the absolute majority of the countries in the world, even if here some discrepancies exist between the two nationalities: US citizens need visas to travel to Iran and Brazil, for instance, while these destinations are visa-free for the Europeans. The EU and the US are similar in that plenty of countries around the world whose own citizens cannot visit the US or the Schengen area without a visa do not apply reciprocity to EU and US citizens, reflecting the power balance in the contemporary world.

In a way, even though EU nationality always comes above the US in the QNI, it is still somewhat undervalued in the QNI, since the value of the US nationality is counted in the QNI on the assumption that the EU is a combination of 28 Member States. Should the value be recounted replacing visa-free travel to 28 EU states with one (the EU), which would be most logical for the purposes of our thought experiment, the gap between the quality of the US and EU nationalities would increase greatly.

The Commonwealth of Independent States Region

Greg Nizhnikaŭ
Skytte Institute,
University of Tartu,
Estonia

The CIS region consists of the 12 former Soviet Republics (except the Baltic States), which belong(ed) to the Commonwealth of Independent States – a regional organization in the post-soviet space.[21] The countries in this region belong to two different and competing regional integration processes. First, the Russia-led Eurasian Economic Union (EaU), which is the economic union of Armenia, Belarus, Kazakhstan, Kyrgyzstan and Russia with free movement of goods, capital, services and people and common transport, agriculture and energy policies. Since its inauguration in 2015, it succeeded the Russia-created Customs Union. Second, the EU's bilateral political and economic association agreements concluded with Moldova, Ukraine and Georgia within the framework of the European Neighbourhood Policy aiming at integrating the EU's neighbors into EU's legal and economic space.

With the exception of Russian nationality (which has a high quality), the CIS nationalities belong to the medium quality tier of the QNI. They can be divided into two groups on their travel and settlement rights: among which the citizens of the first one – consisting of Belarus, Ukraine, Russia, Moldova and Kazakhstan – enjoy more rights than their South Caucasian and Central Asian counterparts, which comprise the second group. In the CIS, key destination countries are Russia and Kazakhstan for Central Asian nationalities. Key source countries are Moldova, Ukraine, Uzbekistan and Tajikistan. The biggest progress between 2011 and 2015 has been achieved by Moldova (moving from 88th to 77th), while Russian and Turkmenistan

21   It includes Armenia, Azerbaijan, Belarus, Kazakhstan, Kyrgyzstan, Moldova, Russia, Uzbekistan, Tajikistan, Turk-
       menistan and Ukraine. Georgia has not formally been a CIS member since 2009, having left it after the Russian–
       Georgian war in 2008, yet it is considered to be a part of the CIS region

citizens have by far the best (from 64th to 60th position) and the worst (from 115th to 123rd) nationalities. The countries in the first group in general also enjoy better Internal Value scores, which explain their similarly higher positions in the QNI General Ranking.

While travel is visa-free among CIS countries except for some notable exceptions (for example, Georgians travelling to Russia), settlement policies in the CIS region are characterized by a significant level of protection of the national labor markets. The regimes in CIS countries vary from all-free-to-work countries like Georgia to the fully restricted Turkmenistan, however the rest of the CIS countries have special quotas for foreign labor force and oblige potential foreign workers to obtain permits to settle. The overall tendency in the region during 2011 and 2015 has been to improve the regulatory access to the national labor markets. The Russia-created regional integration processes – the Customs Union (2011) and the Eurasian Economic Union (2015) include a provision for a free movement of labor. For example, the Treaty on the Eurasian Economic Union states that from 1 January 2015, employers are allowed to hire any citizens of Member States of the EaU regardless of the existing protection measures of the national labor markets. This provision became particularly important for CIS countries since Russia, which is the main destination for labor migration in the region, changed its migration laws to prevent granting *de facto* permanent residence to citizens of visa-free countries. As a result, for example, Tajikistan's nationality dropped on the External Value Ranking from 18.1 (104th) to 15.6% (107th) in 2015 and Ukraine's from 25.3% (82nd) to 22.7% (86th). Besides boosting regional integration, the changes between 2011 and 2015 were driven by the necessity to fix the disorganized state of regulation in work permits and the necessity to tackle illegal work migration. Using existing loopholes caused by the obsolete laws and managements systems, which allowed the automatic prolonging of residence after 90 days upon arrival in Russia or Ukraine, the majority of foreign workers have been "illegally" employed in countries like Kazakhstan and Russia. Yet, the willingness to legalize at least a part of the illegal workforce turned into additional restrictions for employment (as in Russia). For instance, the Uzbek nationality's External Value score has decreased from 18.7% in 2014 (102nd) to 15.9% in 2015 (105th).

This tendency was partly conditioned by the EU policies towards Moldova, Georgia, and Ukraine, which has been driven by the aspiration of these countries to arrange a visa-free regime with the EU. This required the re-organization of the migration sector and a stricter enforcement of rules through bilaterally agreed Visa Liberalisation Action Plans. Among the CIS countries, Russian nationals enjoy the freest regime to travel and settle. Its External Value has particularly grown from 25.7% in 2011 (70th) to 31.1% in 2015 (58th) on the External Value Ranking. This has been accompanied by the steady growth of Travel Freedom of its nationals during that period (from 42.7% in 2011 (71st) to 50.2% in 2015 (68th) on the Travel Freedom Ranking) due to the conclusion of bilateral visa-free agreements with a number of countries during that period (for example, from Gambia to Paraguay).

Similar tendencies are observed in other EaU countries, in particular Belarus (82nd on the 2015 QNI General Ranking) and Kazakhstan (83rd on the 2015 QNI General Ranking), which offer a free right to settle for each other's citizens. Belarus follows Russia in the general ranking due to its high Internal Value, yet its External Value remains stable between 2011 and 2015, recording a slight growth from 21.4% (84th) to 22.7% (86th). It can be explained by the fact that Belarusians' right to settle in some post-soviet countries was attained before the activation of the regional integration processes, while it showed lack of interest in other initiatives, such as visa liberalization with the EU. Kazakhstan has improved steadily, catching up with Belarus and Ukraine on its External Value. Ukraine's rating (87th on the 2015 QNI General Ranking) has improved significantly in 2013, yet Russia's decision to review its settlement rights to non-EaU citizens was one of the reasons for decreasing the high score of its External Value from 25.3% to 22.7% in 2015.

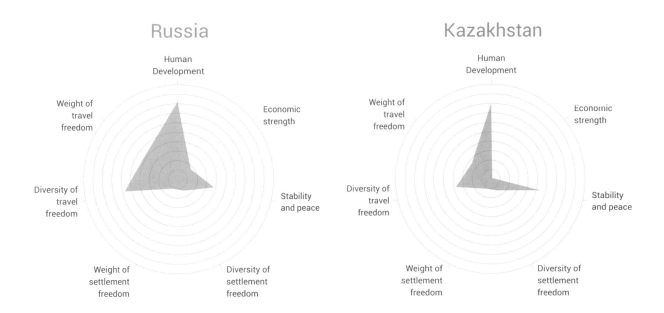

In this light, it should be noted that the policies of Russia play a significant role in explaining the tendencies in the region. The Russian Federation is the main destination for work migration for citizens of post-soviet countries, yet since 2015 it has provided unrestricted labor access exclusively for members of the Customs Union / Eurasian Union – Belarus (since 2011), Kazakhstan (since 2012), Kyrgyzstan (2015) and Armenia (2014) as well as for the asylum-seekers from Ukraine's Donetsk and Luhansk regions. In general, between 2011 and 2015, Russia's work permit regime has evolved towards a more restrictive one, which coincided with growing domestic anti-immigration sentiments and the development of its regional integration projects – the Customs Union and the Eurasian Union.

Firstly, since 2014, Russia – the biggest settlement and travel destination for CIS citizens – has tightened up its residence rules for immigrants from visa-free countries who arrive without a work permit. Foreigners with the right to visa-free entry to Russia may reside on its territory for a maximum of 90 days within a half-year period. Until 2014, the citizens of visa-free (CIS) countries had a *de facto* permanent residence permit, as they could remain on Russian territory for 90 days without any further time restrictions, which therefore allowed them to return to Russia the following day after a 90 day period without losing the right to legal residence.

Secondly, since 2015, the mandatory permit system for all foreign labor workers from visa-free countries was introduced except for EaU nationalities, which carries considerable expenses for its potential seekers. It obliges the workers from CIS countries to hold a work permit. To obtain a work permit, the applicant must register with the Migration Service within 30 days of arrival in the country, pass a medical check, buy insurance, receive an identification tax number, pass an exam on knowledge of the Russian language, history and legislation, and pay a monthly fee. Altogether, with indirect fees, the total cost is estimated to be approximately EUR 450.

These Russian policies were a part of an incentive package to make its integration processes more attractive and partially as a punishing reaction to the visa liberalization processes that has been initiated by the EU with Georgia, Ukraine and Moldova, aimed at preparing them for visa-free travel. The visa-free regime is considered to be one of the biggest attractions for post-Soviet countries to integrate further with the EU. In this regard, Moldova's most significant progress in the region is explained by its entry into the EU visa-free travel regime in 2014. Moldovans, of whom approximately half a million already have Romanian nationality,[22] were granted the right to reside for three months in a 180 day period in the Schengen area, which led to a significant increase of its score on the External Value Ranking by almost 7% to 27.0 in 2015 (from 94th to 71st place).

Finally, the citizens of the South Caucasus republics as well as the Central Asian republics which already belong to the second tier of CIS countries with the worst nationalities in the CIS region based on their External Values range from the lowest External Value Ranking score of 11.2% by Turkmenistan (128th) to the highest of 17.5% by Georgia in 2015 (99th). They have been similarly affected by the Russia's new policies, which led to some deterioration in their External Value in 2015. The Central Asian republics were also affected by the decision of Kazakhstan, which has more than one million citizens of Uzbekistan, Tajikistan, and Kyrgyzstan registered in the country, to grant work permits for visa-free countries only to provide household services to individuals. Yet, both Georgia and Ukraine have significant potential to improve their External Value in the near future due to the process of implementing the Visa Liberalisation Action Plan with the EU. Most of the nationalities in the CIS region have shown some increase in their External Values since 2011. Russia and Moldova are the leaders in the region and are followed by Kazakhstan (22.2%), Belarus and Ukraine (both 22.7%). South Caucasian and Central Asian republics continue to lag significantly behind (11.2 to 17.5%). The overall increase is explained by the growing regional integration tendencies in the post-Soviet space. In 2015, the countries outside the Russia-led integration projects experienced some decrease in scores due to the growing tendency of Russia and Kazakhstan − the biggest destination countries − to protect their national labor markets from the nationalities of non-members of the EaU. Moldova was the only exception due to of its acceptance into the EU visa-free regime.

22   http://www.osw.waw.pl/en/publikacje/analyses/2015-05-06/moldova-a-year-after-introduction-visa-free-regime

South American Nationalities

*Diego Acosta Arcarazo
Jean Monnet Centre,
NYU Law School; University
of Bristol Law School*

South America consists of 12 States which belong to the very high (Chile and Argentina), high (Brazil, Uruguay, Paraguay, Venezuela, and Peru) and medium (Ecuador, Bolivia, Colombia, Suriname, and Guyana) tiers of the QNI. Their situation has either improved or remained stable in the period of 2011 to 2015, due to a number of developments explained below.

Migration and mobility have been the object of legislative and political attention since the independence of the former colonies from Spain and Portugal at the beginning of the 19th century. From the very early stages, the new States signed bilateral and multilateral agreements facilitating free movement and equal treatment of regional nationals. Several of these countries also enshrined constitutional provisions which included principles such as open borders, access to equal rights for foreigners in general, and preferential treatment to naturalize for Hispano-American nationals. With the turn from the 19th to the 20th century, and due to a variety of reasons, many of these legislative choices became less liberal. Despite this restrictive turn, there were continuous discussions and treaties signed on common consular protection abroad, access to civil rights, and recognition of professional qualifications.

During the last 50 years, free movement has been mainly debated within the framework of regional organizations. The Andean Community was founded in 1969 with the Cartagena Treaty. During the 1970s it included six countries: Bolivia, Colombia, Ecuador, Peru, Chile and Venezuela. The last two withdrew their membership in 1976 and 2006 respectively. In turn, MERCOSUR was founded with the Asuncion Treaty in 1991. Its members are Argentina, Bolivia, Brazil, Paraguay, Uruguay and Venezuela (which joined in 2012). The remaining six countries in South America are Associate States which means that they can also implement legislation adopted at the MERCOSUR level. This is the case for the MERCOSUR Residence Agreement, the most important mobility treaty in the region, which will be analyzed below.

At a discursive level, the South American Conference on Migration (SCM)[23] has dealt with the issue since 2001, when it started discussing the free movement of people as part of a new international reality including regional integration and globalization.[24] Consequently, the need to promote free movement of people in the region has been a favorite of the Conference´s final decla-rations,[25] with a special emphasis in the last five years, notably in the 2011 final declaration in Brazil, eloquently entitled "towards a South American citizenship".

Current Legislation on Free Movement and Equal Treatment

Within this regional framework two aspects must be distinguished: free movement for short stays under 90 days, usually associated with tourism or business purposes, and free move-ment in order to reside and/or work.

With reference to the Andean Community, Andean nationals can move with passports by simply presenting their national identity cards. They may remain in another Member State's territory for a period of up to 90 days, renewable for another 90. Andean nationals also enjoy a common passport as well as consular protection abroad from any of the Member State's authorities in case of not having diplomatic representation from their country in the particular state where they find themselves.[26] They also enjoy non-discrimination due to nationality in access to the labor market and equal access to social security.[27]

At the level of MERCOSUR there are also agreements regarding travel documents.[28] However the most important legislation is the 2002 MERCOSUR Residence Agreement. Implemented in 2009, the Agreement's main objective is dealing with the situation of intra-regional migrants and it has transformed the migration regime for South Americans. It provides that any national of a MER-COSUR or Associate Member State may reside and work for a period of two years in a host State with the only requirement of the absence of a criminal record and proof of nationality. Natural-ized citizens in one of the Member States need to wait for five years before they can move. After

23 The South American Conference on Migration is a regional consultative process in which all 12 countries in South America participate. It adopts final declarations that are not legally binding

24 South American Conference on Migration, "Acta de la Comisión. Libre Movilidad de Personas", Santiago de Chile, 2–3 April 2001

25 See final Declarations Montevideo 2003; Montevideo 2008; Quito 2009; Cochabamba 2010; Brasilia 2011; Santia-go 2012; Cartagena 2013 and Lima 2014

26 Andean Community, Decisions 504 and 548

27 Andean Community, Decisions 545, 583 and 584

28 MERCOSUR CMC/DEC. No 37/14

two years, a temporary residence permit may be transformed into a permanent one if the person proves legitimate means of living for his or herself and any family members. It also lays down a number of rights including the right to work and equal treatment in working conditions, family reunion and access to education for children. All countries in South America (i.e., not just MER-COSUR countries) have ratified the agreement and apply it with the exception of Venezuela, where it is currently under discussion, and Surinam and Guyana, where it is yet to be adopted.

Towards a Regional Citizenship?

It is within this historical, political and legal framework that the discussions on establishing a regional citizenship must be understood. On 16 December 2010, the Common Market Council, Mercosur's[29] highest decision-making body, adopted Decision 64/10 on citizenship.[30] Its aim was to establish an action plan to progressively conform a Mercosur citizenship statute to be adopted by 2021, coinciding with the organization's 30th anniversary. This builds on the MER-COSUR Residence Agreement discussed in the previous section. The Andean Community has also debated this subject through its Migration Forum. Discussions have taken place on the possible adoption of an Andean Migration Statute which would consolidate all the current legislation on the subject into one instrument and contribute to the consolidation of an Andean and South American citizenship.[31]

Finally, UNASUR[32] introduced the establishment of a future regional citizenship as one of its aims in its founding treaty, which entered into force on 11 March 2011. Article 3(i) establishes as one of its objectives the consolidation of a South American identity through the progressive

29 Mercosur, the Southern Common Market, is a regional organization in South America comprising Argentina, Brazil, Paraguay (currently suspended in its membership), Uruguay and Venezuela. Bolivia is currently in the process of accession. All other six countries in South America (Bolivia, Chile, Colombia, Ecuador, Guyana, Peru and Surinam) are associate Member States and may as such adhere to Mercosur's agreements. See Common Market Council Decisions 11/13, 18/04 and 28/04

30 MERCOSUR/CMC/DEC. N° 64/10

31 See Bogota Declaration, Andean Migration Forum, 10 May 2013

32 UNASUR, Union of South American Nations, is a regional organization comprising all 12 countries in South America. It aims at constructing a cultural, economic, social and political space in the region

recognition of rights to those nationals of one Member State residing in the territory of another Member State, with the aim of achieving a South American citizenship.[33] The final declarations of the 2012, 2013 and 2014 ordinary meetings of the Council of the Heads of State and Government reinforced the aim of attaining a true South American citizenship as the backbone of an integrated South American space,[34] and proposed to establish a single passport.[35]

The coming period seems an exciting one with regards to the development of regional mobility, equal treatment and, possibly, the establishment of a common citizenship. As the QNI Index clearly depicts, having a South American nationality is now more relevant and valuable thank to the opportunities it brings for mobility among an increasingly larger number of countries. The biggest progress in the general ranking in the period of 2011 to 2015 was achieved by Colombia (from 107th to 81st) and Ecuador (from 90th to 67th). Chilean citizens have the best passport (34th), closely followed by Argentina (37th), Brazil (38th), Uruguay (41st) and Paraguay (47th). This situation could improve further once Venezuela implements the Mercosur Residence agreement in 2016, since it is legally bound by its Mercosur membership to adopt legislation this year at the latest. It could also progress even more if Suriname and Guyana ratified this agreement, although as associate members they are not legally obliged to. Such ratification however would greatly improve their general ranking and value of their passport since it is now the worst in the region (94th and 98th position respectively). Finally, Columbia and Peru recently obtained visa-free travel to the Schengen area, further improving their rankings.

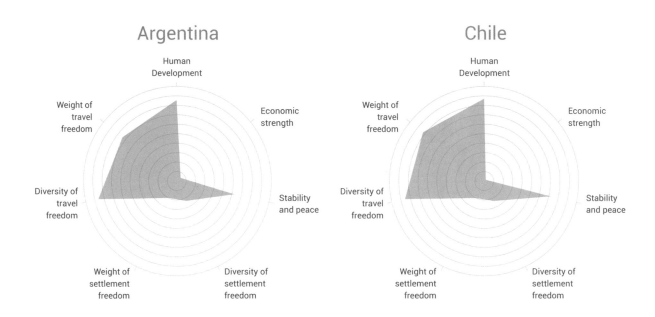

33 This is also mentioned in the preamble as the determination to construct an identity and South American citizen-ship. Article 3(k) also establishes as one of the objectives of this organization the cooperation on migration matters under the strict respect of human and labor rights in order to achieve migration regularization and the harmoniza-tion of policies

34 Declaration of the 6th ordinary meeting of the Council of Heads of State and Government of the UNASUR, Lima, 30 November 2012. Declaration of the 7th ordinary meeting of the Council, Paramaribo, 2 September 2013

35 Declaration of the 8th ordinary meeting of the Council of Heads of State and Government of the UNASUR, Quito 4–5 December, para 14

The Gulf Cooperation Council

Justin Lindeboom
University of Groningen,
The Netherlands

The Gulf Cooperation Council (GCC) is an Arab political and economic organization comprising Bahrain, Kuwait, Oman, Qatar, Saudi Arabia, and the United Arab Emirates. It is one of the few regional organizations offering genuine free settlement for Member State nationals.[36] Since the GCC's foundation in 1981, freedom of mobility and residence has been one of the main objectives to be implemented over time in order to foster the Gulf Arab identity or *khaleeji*.[37] Since 2001, nationals of GCC countries have had a specific right to unrestricted free movement and full access to other Member States. This liberalized regime stands in sharp contrast with highly restrictive migration policies for foreign workers, who comprise a clear majority of the GCC labor workforce. In practice, free movement and settlement rights in the GCC are hardly used by those who have them. By contrast, the lack of overlap between inhabitants and nationals – which is unique in the world – also entails that more than half of the current population of the GCC does not enjoy the key benefits of having a corresponding nationality.

The nationalities of the GCC belong to the lower range of the high-quality tier (Qatar, United Arab Emirates, and Kuwait) and the higher range of the medium-quality tier (Saudi Arabia, Oman, and Bahrain) of the QNI General Ranking. In terms of Internal Value, the GCC nationalities primarily benefit from a relatively high level of Human Development, in particular compared with other nationalities in the Middle East region. The large size of their oil-driven economies does not directly reflect into equivalent value, because revenue from Natural Resources Rents (NRR) is excluded from QNI's calculation of a nationality's Economic Strength. For all of the GCC nationalities, NRR amounts to double-digit percentages of the economy. Indirectly, however, the high level of economic welfare does boost the overall quality of most GCC nationalities through their Human Development scores, particularly pertaining to

36 In addition to the European Union, MERCOSUR, and, to some extent, ECOWAS. On free movement within the EU, see the special contribution by Dimitry Kochenov, pp 140; on MERCOSUR, see the special contribution by Diego Acosta, pp 147; and on ECOWAS, see pp 101

37 Z. Babar, "Free Mobility within the Gulf Cooperation Council" (Center for International and Regional Studies 2011) 3

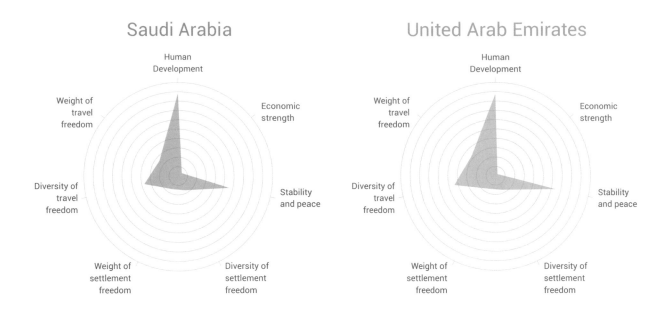

Saudi Arabia

Human
Development

Weight of
travel
freedom

Economic
strength

Diversity of
travel
freedom

Stability
and peace

Weight of
settlement
freedom

Diversity of
settlement
freedom

United Arab Emirates

Human
Development

Weight of
travel
freedom

Economic
strength

Diversity of
travel
freedom

Stability
and peace

Weight of
settlement
freedom

Diversity of
settlement
freedom

countries with a superb GDP per capita like Qatar. Most of the GCC nationalities lost some of their quality between 2011 and 2015 due to regional tensions and instability. This negatively affected the nationalities of Qatar (from 54th to 60th place), the United Arab Emirates (from 59th to 62nd), Kuwait (from 57th to 63rd), Oman (from 60th to 73rd), and Bahrain (from 60th to 75th). Saudi Arabian nationality withstood this trend with a minor increase in Peace and Stability as well as increased visa-free or visa-on-arrival travel freedom for its nationals (from 57 to 65 destinations), resulting in one rank upwards (from 69th to 68th). Despite the negative regional movement, the average value of GCC nationalities on the 2015 QNI General Ranking (35.1%) is substantially higher than the Middle Eastern average (26.5%). Within the region, accordingly, the GCC only leaves Israeli nationality (41.9% at 49th place) ahead. In fact, while the quality of GCC nationalities varies between 37.4% (Qatar) and 33.2% (Bahrain), the next Middle Eastern

  nationality follows at a remarkable distance (Tunisian at 26.9%). This is primarily caused by the free mobility of persons in the GCC area, which boosts Settlement Freedom and overall External Value. Since the Economic Agreement 2001, nationals are even entitled to pensions and social security benefits in other Member States, going beyond the QNI's criteria for full access.

Genuine free movement of nationals is thus one of the more successful pillars of the GCC as a project of regional integration. However, the massive influx of foreign workers in recent decades has substantially diminished the relevance of the GCC free mobility regime for two reasons. Firstly, GCC nationals rarely make use of their free movement rights, while secondly, foreign workers do not have them. The GCC countries are described as "rentier states", which means that most of the government revenues come from rents of natural resources. Consequently, the GCC economies can survive without a strong internal sector, and to a large extent government revenue is distributed among nationals through public sector employment. Meanwhile, since the late 1980s, the private sector has been importing a massive number of non-Arab foreign migrants, most of whom are low-skilled workers from South Asia. As a result, the percentage of GCC nationals working in the private sector remains minimal, despite multiple attempts of labor nationalization with little to mixed results.[38] In 2011, for example, only 0.5% of the private workforce in Qatar was Qatari nationals.[39]

Even taking into account the public sector, employment figures among nationals are low. Unemployment rates are generally above 10%[40] and youth unemployment can be up to 30% in for example Saudi Arabia.[41] Labor force participation rates are much lower even. Both in Saudi Arabia and Qatar, nationals who were employed accounted for only one-fifth of the total national population, which is one of the lowest dependence ratios worldwide.[42] In Kuwait, this ratio is only comparatively high with a participation rate of about one-third of national population.[43]

Given the uniquely low labor activity of GCC nationals in comparison to foreign workers, it will come as no surprise that employment of GCC nationals in Member States other than their country of origin is marginal. Though recent statistics are not easily available, it is estimated that in 2010 only 21,000 GCC nationals were working in another GCC Member State, equal to 1.7% of the total active national labor force. There are measurable differences among the GCC nationalities, which roughly reflect the divergences in national welfare and economic opportunities, as well as the overall quality of nationalities. The limited amount of intra-regional labor mobility flows largely from countries of the lower-ranking GCC nationalities towards countries of the higher-ranking ones. Nationals from Bahrain (75th on the QNI General Ranking), Oman (73rd), and Saudi Arabia (68th) are most likely to work in other GCC countries, while those from Kuwait (63rd), the United Arab Emirates (62nd), and Qatar (60th) make practically no use of their free movement rights at all. Correspondingly, the United Arab Emirates and Qatar are the most attractive destinations in the region, and Bahrain and Oman by far the least attractive.[44]

38 K. Randeree, "Workforce Nationalization in the Gulf Cooperation Council States" (Center for International and Regional Studies 2012)

39 "Country Profile No 25: The Gulf Cooperation Council States (GCC)" (Focus Migration, Institute for Migration Research and Intercultural Studies, December 2012), 6

40 Babar, "Free Mobility", 21

41 "Country Profile No 25", 7

42 Ibid., 6

43 G. Naufal and I. Genc, "Labor Migration in the GCC Countries: Past, Present and Future" (2014) Singapore Middle East Papers No 9/2, 17

44 B.A. Ibrahim, "Intra-National Labour Mobility among the Arab Gulf Cooperation Council States in the Context of the Financial Crisis and the Gulf Monetary Union" in Intra-Regional Labour Mobility in the Arab World (International Organization for Migration 2010) 108, 122–123

The salient disinterest of GCC nationals in using the key benefit of their nationalities' External Value is partly explained by factors including higher employment opportunities for natives, low educational levels, and strong family ties.[45] However, also the influx of migrant workers occupying the vast majority of private sector work significantly hampers employment opportunities both within and outside people's country of origin.

The number of foreign workers in the Gulf countries has increased continuously during the past decades and was estimated to exceed 30 million in 2014, which is equivalent to 62% of the GCC's total population. These numbers vary largely among the Gulf countries, from 32.4% foreign inhabitants in Saudi Arabia to 85.7% in Qatar and 88.5% in the United Arab Emirates.[46] It is however absolutely clear that migrants have an overwhelming presence in the private labor market, which far exceeds the share of foreign workers in high-immigration OECD countries such as Australia and New Zealand. Unlike GCC nationals, the group of over 30 million foreign workers is confronted with tight migration policies. Entry and exit into the territories is strictly controlled, and low-skilled foreign workers are generally kept separate from the rest of the society. In the construction and agriculture sectors, such low-skilled migrants often require permission of their employers to leave the country or move to a new job.

The GCC countries have given several justifications for their tight migration rules for foreign workers. These reasons include internal security and stability, the preservation of cultural homogeneity and the Arab identity, and the protection of employment for nationals.[47] Meanwhile, the Gulf's private sector economy remains heavily dependent upon a foreign workforce. The sharp contrast between unrestricted freedom of movement and residence of GCC nationals on the one hand, and a complete lack of such freedom for foreign workers on the other, will thus most likely remain in place in the near future.

Accordingly, free mobility in the GCC is in many respects a peculiar regime. Usually the rationale for free movement of persons across borders centers on either moral or economic arguments. Neither of the two seems to fit the GCC: while nationals rarely use their free movement rights at all, if only because labor participation is extremely low, foreign workers who could actually benefit from free mobility are deprived of any comparable right to regional free movement. Far more than in moral or economic justifications, free mobility in the Gulf area seems rooted in the idea of fostering the *khaleeji* identity. As a result, however, the GCC has until now ended up with a partly liberalized regime of free movement that is received with remarkable disinterest among citizens, while more than half of the current population cannot use it anyway.

---

45 Ibid., 123–124

46 Naufal and Genc, 'Labor Migration', 11–12

47 See Babar, 'Free Mobility', 15–24

The Pacific Region

Gerard Prinsen
School of People,
Environment and Planning,
Massey University,
New Zealand

When endeavoring to rank the quality of nationalities – as legal statuses of attachment to states – in the Pacific, two challenges emerge. First, there is no clear line dividing Pacific islands into states – defined as "sovereign territorial entities" earlier in the QNI – and non-sovereign territories. Instead, the Pacific region's islands are better understood when placed on a continuum with sovereign states on one end of the scale and, on the other end, islands that are overseas territories of states that are located thousands of miles away. Examples of islands that are sovereign states would be Tonga, Fiji, or Papua New Guinea. Examples of Pacific islands whose nationality is taken from sovereign states thousands of miles away would be Hawaii's (from the US), Rapa Nui (from Chile), or New Caledonia (from France). In between these two extreme ends lies an array of islands that have very diverse constitutional and legal arrangements that continue to tie them to the Pacific's (former) colonial metropoles: France, the US, and New Zealand. As a consequence, assessing the external value of these nationalities for the purpose of the QNI would need to be done on a case-by-case basis.

A few examples illustrate the uniqueness of each nationality of the territories in the middle section of that continuum. American Samoa is legally defined as an "unincorporated territory of the US" and this leaves its people with an American passport imprinted with the message "The bearer of this passport is a US national and not a US citizen". These passport-holders have the right to reside in the US, but they cannot vote. They are entitled to enroll in the US army (they have, in fact, the highest rate of military enlistment of any US territory), but they cannot own concealed

An inscription in an American Samoa-issued US passport specifying that the bearer is a US national without citizenship.

weapons and are excluded from most government employment opportunities. The island state of Guam, on the other hand, is legally defined as an "unincorporated and organized territory of the US" and their US passport has no residence or employment restrictions, although some of their civil rights are curtailed. (They can, for example, elect a senator to the US House of Representatives, but this senator's status is reduced to that of a "a non-voting delegate").

Another example to illustrate the uniqueness of many Pacific nationalities is the Niuean nationality. Niue is a self-governing state in free association with New Zealand. People on Niue hold dual citizenship; they are also entitled to a New Zealand passport and the associated citizenship entitlements, provided they apply for the passport in New Zealand. If they acquire Niuean citizenship in Niue, that document does not automatically transfer into a New Zealand passport. Moreover, the arrangement is not mutual and a New Zealand passport does not entitle the holder to rights on Niue that Niuean citizens have. Practically, this means not only restrictions to residence and employment on Niue, but also that travelers to Niue need to buy a return airfare unless they prove they are Niuean by birth or the descendant of a Niuean. The Cook Islands, another country in free association with New Zealand, do not issue their own citizenship document, but they have detailed specific regulations with regard to residence, investment, and employment on the islands. A permanent residence permit requires a ten year residence, (three years for New Zealand citizens) and an individual assessment.

In essence, these examples show that in the Pacific region, the terms and benefits of a nationality of a territory are often distinguished from the terms and benefits of citizenship of the same territory. This complicates an assessment of the two external aspects of the QNI General Ranking – Travel Freedom and Settlement Freedom – for each Pacific nationality. Nonetheless, a few patterns can be noted for each aspect. With regard to travel freedom, the Pacific region is divided into two distinct groups of nations. On the one side, there are the islands whose people carry passports of their (former) colonial metropoles and they possess the associated travel freedom, all ranking in the top tier of the QNI General Ranking. People from French Polynesia, New Caledonia, and Wallis and Futuna benefit from France's high ranking of 7th out of 161 in the QNI. Followed at some distance, but still within the same top tier, are citizens of American Samoa, Guam, and the Northern Mariana Islands who travel on a US passport which is ranked 28th; followed closely by people from the Cook Islands, Niue, and Tokelau who travel on a New Zealand passport, ranked 31st. On the other side, nearly in the lowest tier of the QNI, is the freedom of travel for people with a Papua New Guinea nationality, ranked 119th.

The travel freedom of citizens of the Federated States of Micronesia, the Marshall Islands, and Palau has not (yet) been ranked in the QNI, due to a lack of exact information. It is worth noting though that while people from these islands travel on their own national passports, the current conditions of their countries' Compact of Free Association with the US enable them to enter the US visa-free as "non-immigrants". Their travel freedom to other countries will vary and be subject to particular arrangements. What also remains is an assessment of the travel freedom of the other independent countries in the Pacific region: Fiji, Kiribati, Nauru, Samoa, Solomon Islands, Tonga, Tuvalu, and Vanuatu. As noted earlier in the report; for this 2015 edition, these nationalities have been excluded while detailed information is being gathered and assessed.

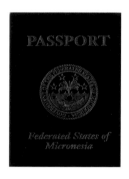 

For Settlement Freedom, it needs to be noted that residence conditions are often differentiated between settlement in the (former) colonial metropole and settlement in the Pacific island's territory. The former – migration from the Pacific islands into New Zealand, Australia, or the US – is an important feature of economic and demographic dynamics in the Pacific. In many cases, more islanders reside in the metropoles than in the territories themselves. There are, for example, three times more Cook Islanders residing in New Zealand than on the Cook Islands. Auckland is described as having the largest concentration of Polynesians in the world. The latter – migration into Pacific islands – is often subject to several conditions that vary throughout the Pacific, but often considers birthplace and family lineage. By extension, the possibilities for private investment in and ownership of land in most Pacific territories are generally subject to legal restrictions and influenced strongly by local cultural practices.

In addition, it should be noted that where Pacific territories retain constitutional and legal arrangements with their (former) colonial metropoles of France, the US and New Zealand, these arrangements are often subject to repeated or continuous renegotiations between each individual territory and the metropole. These renegotiations affect the conditions of travel and settlement associated with the Pacific territories involved. New Caledonia, for example, has had ten different constitutional arrangements with France since 1946, leading some analysts to speak of the "waltz of statuses" or the "institutional yo-yo". This has implications for the quality of nationality in New Caledonia, even if all people living in New Caledonia are French citizens. In particular, the latest round of renegotiation – resulting in the Nouméa Agreement of 1998 – differentiates voting and employment conditions between, on the one hand, the territory's indigenous population and those on the electoral roll before 1998 and, on the other hand, the people who arrived or enrolled later. An upcoming referendum on independence is to be organized before 2018. This will, undoubtedly, trigger another series of changes that affect the quality of nationality and citizenship in New Caledonia.

After the complexities that result from the differentiation between nationality and citizenship in the Pacific, the second challenge in ranking the Pacific's nationalities results from the fact that many of the Pacific's territories have rather small populations and limited capacities of public services. This means the public data on these territories is often too limited to make an assessment of the internal value of the quality of their nationality for the QNI. To illustrate this challenge, a brief look at population size of the Pacific territories suffices. Once the three largest Pacific nations are excluded (Australia, Papua New Guinea, and New Zealand), there are no Pacific territories with a population over one million people. In fact, once Fiji and the Solomon Islands are also excluded, all the remaining twenty-something territories have populations of less than 300,000. Inevitably, many of these territories do not have, or do not publish reliable data on their GDP and international bodies overlook or omit them in their ranking – as is the case with the Human Development Index and the Global Peace Index.

Pacific territories have been undertaking several initiatives to deal with the challenge of small populations, limited public services, and regional collaboration. Two of these initiatives are likely to grow in relevance and may, eventually, impinge on the quality of the nationality of its members. First, the Pacific Island Forum was established as the South Pacific Forum in 1971, but expanded its mandate and membership in the 2000s. Its membership now includes 16 independent and self-governing states and a handful of associate members and observers – reflecting the continuum of shades of sovereignty mentioned earlier. Most of its activities are directed at inter-governmental cooperation and international representation; issues of nationality and citizenship do not really feature. Similarly, a second regional initiative is the Melanesian Spearhead Group, founded in 1986 by Fiji, Papua New Guinea, the Solomon Islands, Vanuatu, and the political party representing the indigenous people of New Caledonia. As from 2007, it began expanding its mandate and membership too, focusing more on trade and exchange between members. Both these initiatives for regional collaboration have the potential to improve the internal value of their members' nationalities by increasing economic opportunities and reducing risks from poor governance and domestic conflict. However, there are no clear signs that these two initiatives for regional collaboration are considering enhancing freedom or choice in travel and settlement which would increase the External Value of their members' nationalities.

Australia

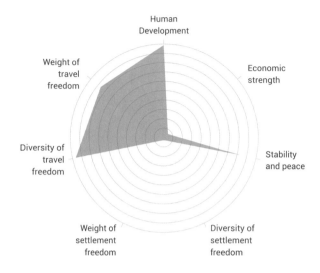

Papua New Guinea

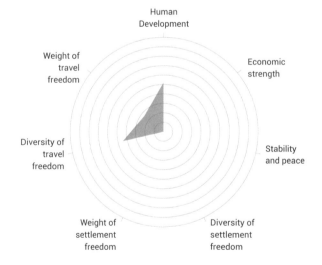

China and India

Suryapratim Roy
School of Law,
Trinity College Dublin

China and India have been in the international spotlight for the last two decades, primarily due to the spectacular speed of their economic growth and robust cross-border financial flows. In the World Bank estimates of GDP growth, India and China are tied at a compelling 7.3% annual growth rate between 2011 and 2015. This directly translates into the Economic Strength component of the QNI, which constitutes 15% of the ranking. It could be suggested that there are be myriad ways in which Economic Strength may have an indirect effect on the other sub-elements of the QNI. It transpires from the cumulative ranking that such indirect effects are not evident, and in the case of India probably modest: China secures a rank of 60 and India 102. The two countries are also outperformed by the majority of other members of the G20, with China ranked at 14 and India at 18. This may be attributed to little progress having been made in relation to other elements of the QNI.

The other beguiling property common to China and India is their size: they encompass several metaphorical nationalities within their borders. Given the internal ethnic diversity within the two countries, there is substantial truth to this perception. This metaphor assumes a literal quality with regard to China – several passports are issued within Chinese territory, corresponding to different legal statuses of belonging known in Chinese law. Importantly, these passports are not ranked equally on the QNI. In fact the "China" mentioned above refers to the People's Republic of China (PRC), and does not include Hong Kong, Macao and Taiwan. All three nationalities rank higher than PRC on the QNI: 45 for Hong Kong, 46 for Taiwan and 52 for Macao. To summarize the status of citizenship in China, a Taiwanese passport is a Republic of China passport. This is distinct from a PRC passport. Permanent Residents of Hong Kong and Macao are eligible for PRC Special Administrative Region (SAR) passports issued under the Basic Laws of Hong Kong SAR and Macao SAR respectively. It may be noted that rules and regulations governing residence and citizenship of Hong Kong and Macao need to be in conformity with the constitution of the PRC. In comparison, post-independence, and after its break from Pakistan and Bangladesh, India issues a single passport, corresponding to one legal status of belonging to the Indian state.

Both India and PRC demonstrate a minor improvement in the cumulative scores that constitute the QNI between 2011 and 2015. PRC has seen a positive change in its value by 4.1 and India by 1.4. This is due to an improvement in the Internal Value of the two nationalities, while Travel and Settlement Freedoms have remained mostly unchanged. Despite similarities in both Economic Strength and Peace and Stability, the comparatively higher Internal Value of China against India may be attributed to its position on the Human Development Index. PRC clocks in at 90th with India at 130th, with an improvement of 13 places for China between 2009 and 2014, and 6 for India. This difference in positions is not recent: an examination of Human Development Reports over the years reveals that there has always been a difference, and that the gap has increased over time. India faces a comparative disadvantage due to its internal disparity: some states such as Kerala may be grouped within very high development nationalities, while others such as Chhattisgarh exhibit properties akin to low development nationalities (UNDP India 2011).

In this regard, the "several nationalities within one country" provides China a distinct advantage. All three associated nationalities – Taiwan, Macao and Hong Kong – outperform mainland China with regard to Human Development. The Economic Strength and Human Development of these countries enhance the weighted Travel and Settlement Freedoms of the countries that have access to them. This potential has been tapped in relation to Travel Freedom by virtue of an Entry and Exit Permit issued to citizens of the PRC for entry into Taiwan, and the PRC's relaxation of visa restrictions on Taiwanese citizens in July 2015. Historically, there have been tensions regarding the autonomy of Hong Kong, Macao and Taiwan on the one hand and attempts at PRC unification on the other. This has resulted in some co-operative freedoms with regard to travel and settlement between PRC, Macao and Hong Kong. Such co-operative freedoms are bested by the travel freedoms enjoyed by Taiwan. The period between 2011 and 2015 was particularly significant for Taiwan due to a visa exemption policy for short-term access to the Schengen area, resulting in a positive change in its QNI value by 13.1. This change, fuelled by trade relations between Taiwan and the EU, positions Taiwan as the highest performing country among all nationalities during this period. Taiwan's position on the QNI is predicted to go higher in future, given the PRC's new policy on allowing entry to Taiwanese citizens mentioned above. In this regard, India still continues to restrict entry of its neighbors (other than Nepal and Bhutan).

An Indian passport, for example, only grants visa-free or visa-on-arrival access to 52 countries and is easily surpassed by countries with lower economic strength such as Bulgaria, with visa-free or visa-on arrival access to 149 countries. We anticipate, however, that there will be some improvement in India's position in subsequent editions of the QNI. This would be due to the ongoing extension of its fast-track e-visa to several countries, which commenced in 2013. This is a much needed improvement; as reciprocity is an important marker in easing the process of international travel, the difficulty in accessing India may be a contributing factor to the difficulty of Indians accessing other countries. The e-visa, however, is restricted to short term visits and is not useful for making inroads into the Indian labor market.

Picking up on concerns informing access to markets, the only sub-element where India performs marginally better than China, Macao, Hong Kong and Taiwan is Settlement Freedom, due to the access of Indian citizens to Nepal. Given that Nepal does not score well on Weighted Settlement Freedom, this advantage is marginal. The QNI clearly indicates that that holders of passports in most countries in South Asia and South-East Asia are not welcome to settle in other countries despite their recent economic performance, and their so-called cultural "soft power". Thus, international migration flows from China and India are relatively high despite low Travel and Settlement Freedoms. As is evident in other segments of this report, the way a country is positioned within regional arrangements has an impact on the value of its nationality on the QNI. By virtue of their position as Member States of the EU, countries acquire a substantially higher value in relation to both Travel Freedom and Settlement Freedom. The association of some post-Soviet republics with Russia has had a varied impact on the value of their nationalities. In comparison, there are relatively little advantages to Settlement Freedoms that India and China can derive from the blocs they find themselves in. This may be understood in relation to (i), postcolonial arrangements, and (ii), arrangements among these countries.

With regard to (i), it is evident that several nationalities derive significant Travel and Settlement Freedoms from their colonial past. We may take, for instance, the Spanish Law of Historical Memory, where travel and settlement in Spain is relaxed for citizens of countries who can demonstrate a link with its colonial past. This does not translate into a QNI advantage, however, since it is not unconditional. Without any doubt, however, decolonization has not been a Travel and Settlement Freedom-enhancing political event for either India or China. Other political events such as wars or the disintegration of an empire have not set in motion processes that enhance the value of their nationalities. In relation to (ii), unlike advantages of travel and settlement available between Taiwan and China, or facilitated by other regional blocs such as the European Union or CIS, there are no such arrangements between India and China. The groups that India and China are categorized under such as BRICS and the G20 do not contribute to their Travel and Settlement Freedoms. The membership of India in arrangements such as the South Asian Association of Regional Cooperation (SAARC) does not mediate either its travel or settlement freedom. This explains why the countries with relatively high travel freedom, namely Hong Kong and Taiwan, have sought out bilateral arrangements.

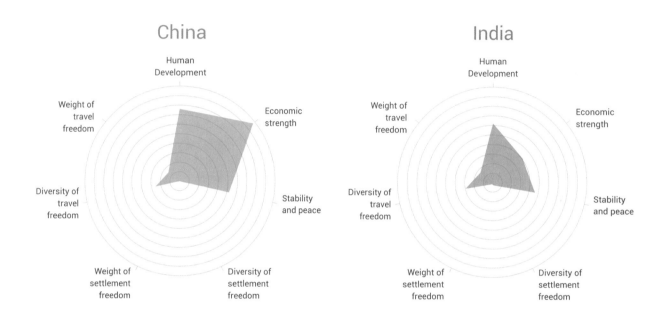

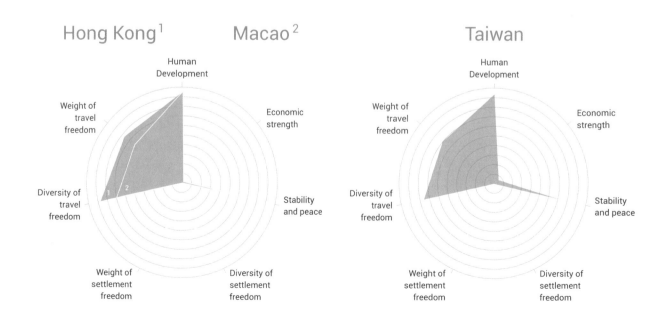

Georgia

*Laure Delcour
Fondation Maison
des Sciences de l'Homme,
France*

Georgia, a post-Soviet country, has developed the most welcoming migration policy in the world, combined with an extremely liberal visa regime. Yet this open policy is in sharp contrast to the way in which Georgian citizens are treated worldwide: Georgia indeed belongs to the medium quality tier of the QNI. Over the past five years, it has consistently been ranked around the 105th position, achieving only limited progress between 2011 (106th) and 2015 (103rd). Among post-Soviet countries, only four Central Asia republics (Turkmenistan, Tajikistan and Kyrghyzstan from 2012 onwards and Uzbekistan after 2013) have ranked behind Georgia, while Kazakhstan has consistently done better. Armenia and Azerbaijan, Georgia's South Caucasus neighbors, are also better positioned in the QNI.

Georgia ranks low by all QNI indicators, yet the country's position is comparatively worse in terms of settlement freedom. Among post-Soviet countries, only Turkmenistan has consistently done worse between 2011 and 2014. However, Georgia's position has improved in 2015. The country has surpassed four of the five Central Asian republics, but also Armenia and Ukraine. In terms of travel freedom, Georgia has ranked between the 99th and 105th position between 2011 and 2015. While the country's position has worsened since 2014, it is better placed than Kyrghyzstan, Turkmenistan, Tajikistan and even neighboring Armenia. Georgian citizens can travel freely (i.e. without a visa or by getting a visa on arrival) to only 62 countries. These are mostly located in the post-Soviet space (with the major exception of Russia), Central and South America and for a few of them Asia (e.g. Turkey; e-visas for India).

Georgia's foreign policy course since the collapse of the Soviet Union carries substantial explanatory weight to account the country's poor performance in terms of quality of nationality. Since the early 1990s, Georgia has been extremely reluctant to engage in any of the regional cooperation or integration schemes gathering post-Soviet states. It joined the Commonwealth of Independent States (CIS) in December 1993, yet withdrew from the CIS Council of Defence Ministers in 2006 and decided to fully withdraw from the organization in the wake of the August 2008 conflict with Russia. Georgia never joined any of the other regional initiatives set up by Russia; for instance, while signing the Collective Security Treaty in 1994, it refrained from renewing its participation in 1999 and did not become a member of the Collective Security Treaty Organisation when the latter was created. Like Turkmenistan (albeit for different reasons), Georgia has therefore remained absent (or at best marginal) in any of the post-Soviet cooperation attempts. This detachment from the post-Soviet space has gone hand in hand with increasingly strained relations with Russia, first over the conflict in Abkhazia and then in the mid-end 1990s over the first conflict in Chechnya. As a consequence, Russia unilaterally introduced a visa obligation on Georgian citizens (with the exception of citizens living in the two secessionist regions of Abkhazia and South Ossetia, who benefited from a simplified border-crossing procedure) in December 2000. In fact, Georgia and Turkmenistan are the only post-Soviet countries that have experienced a visa regime from Russia. The sharp deterioration of relations with Russia after the Rose revolution and the Georgian government's clear prioritization of accession to NATO and the European Union following the Rose Revolution only exacerbated retaliatory actions on the part of Russia. Georgian migrants living in the Russian Federation were massively deported in the wake of the 2006 diplomatic crisis and conditions for obtaining a Russian visa became significantly tougher after the 2008 conflict, not least because of the rupture of diplomatic relations between the two countries.

The limited travel and residence freedom available to Georgian citizens is in sharp contrast to their country's own liberal approach to migrants entering Georgia. Throughout the 2000s, migration was considered a pillar of the authorities' economic strategy, which primarily sought to attract foreign investment and to create a favorable business environment. However, owing to the weak degree of visa, residence and work permits, the country did not comply with EU demands as part of

Passports of unrecognized Russian satellite-states of Abkhazia and South Ossetia

the visa liberalization process. As a result of both increased EU conditionality under the visa liberalization action plan granted to Georgia in early 2013 and the new authorities' more flexible approach to migration, Georgia shifted toward a stricter regulation of migration flows. Yet the law "On the Legal Status of Foreigners and Stateless Persons" that entered into force on 1 September 2014 was sharply criticized as a disincentive for tourism or applying for residence to work, study, or live in the country. While clear-cut visa categories remain in force in line with EU requirements, in May 2015 the Georgian Parliament adopted a package of amendments to the law that re-introduces 360 day visa-free stays for citizens and permanent residents of

94 countries listed in a governmental decree. This demonstrates how deeply entrenched the liberal approach to migration is in Georgian society.

While Georgia has consistently belonged to the medium quality tier of the QNI, this is likely to change in the near future as the result of two processes. Firstly, the visa liberalization process launched with the European Union in 2013 has almost come to an end. In December 2015, the European Commission recommended that the obligation of the Schengen visa be lifted for Georgian citizens. Subject to a decision by the European Parliament and the EU Council of Ministers, a Schengen visa-free regime is expected to materialize mid-2016 for holders of a biometric passport entering the EU. Secondly, as a result of the slow normalization of relations between Georgia and the Russian Federation after the departure of Mikheil Saakashvili, in December 2015 President Putin suggested lifting visa obligations for Georgian citizens travelling to Russia. As a first step toward visa liberalization, the Russian Ministry of Foreign Affairs announced a few days later the facilitation of the visa regime for Georgian citizens. This includes in particular the possibility to issue multiple entry visas for business, work, educational, humanitarian or private purposes. Georgia's ranking is therefore likely to significantly improve as early as 2016.

Georgia

"Non-citizens" of Latvia

Aleksejs Dimitrovs
European Parliament,
Brussels

The legal history of the status of "non-citizens of Latvia" is closely intertwined with the recent past of the State itself. On 15 October 1991 the Latvian Supreme Council (the interim Parliament) passed the Decision "On the Renewal of the Rights of the Citizens of the Republic of Latvia and on the Fundamental Principles of Naturalisation", which was based on the concept of the continuity of the citizenship of the Latvian Republic that existed before the Soviet occupation: only those persons who had been citizens of independent Latvia in 1940 and their descendants had their citizenship restored. This approach was confirmed by the Citizenship Law of 1994.

The legal status of people who were not recognized as citizens of Latvia remained unclear until 1995, when the Law on the Status of Former USSR Citizens Who Do Not Have the Citizenship of Latvia or of Any Other State was adopted. This Law introduced a special legal status of "non-citizens", granted to those who enjoyed registered domicile in Latvia on 1 July 1992 and who did not have citizenship of Latvia or any other country (except for some retired USSR army officers and members of their families). As a result, to this day Latvia knows two statuses, which diverge largely in External Value and overall value. While ordinary Latvian nationality occupies 24th place in the QNI General Ranking, the status of non-citizens ranks 85 places lower at 109th.

According to the clarification by the Latvian Constitutional Court, "non-citizens" "can be regarded neither as citizens, nor as aliens and stateless persons".[48] Latvian and international

---

48 In Latvian: "Latvijas nepilsoņi nav uzskatāmi ne par pilsoņiem, ne ārvalstniekiem, ne arī bezvalstniekiem." See Constitutional Court of Latvia, Case No 2004-15-0106, para 15 (2005), available at *http://www.satv.tiesa.gov.lv/upload/2004- 15-0106E.rtf*

courts clarified that this status amounts to a permanent legal bond between the Latvian Republic and its "non-citizens", thus excluding statelessness.[49]

This status is now held by more than 250,000 people belonging to ethnic minorities – a large share of the population of a tiny state (11.7%) – and this situation is permanent: "non-citizens" are born every day.

Moreover, Latvian law in some cases allows foreign national parents to register their child as a "noncitizen".[50] "Non-citizens" have rights akin to citizens. These include, for example, the right to reside in Latvia without visas or residence permits, the right to work without a work permit, etc. Some rights and opportunities are reserved, however, only for "full" citizens. This includes political rights (such as the right to participate in elections and the right to establish political parties), the right to hold certain government positions, and social and economic rights (land property rights in some territories, public and private sector careers in some professions, pensions for work periods accrued during the Soviet period outside Latvia, if the period is not covered by an international agreement).[51] As of October 2011, there were as many as 80 differences in rights between citizens and "non-citizens", mainly relating to careers in the public sector. The absolute majority persists to this day. In particular, the citizens of Latvia can travel visa-free to 158 states and territories for tourist or business purposes, while non-citizens only to 44. As a result, Latvian nationality occupies 29th place on the 2015 Travel Freedom Ranking, while the status of non-citizens follows at a great distance in 131st place.

Moreover, unlike Latvian nationals, the non-citizens of Latvia enjoy no free movement rights in the EU. In the 2015 Settlement Freedom Ranking, Latvian nationality has a full 100.0% score. By contrast non-citizens have no settlement rights anywhere and are at the bottom of the ranking. This image is replicated in the combined External Value Ranking (Latvian nationality with 93.9% in 18th place, and the status of non-citizens with 11.2% at 128th). As mentioned above, this entails that on the QNI General Ranking, Latvian nationality has a value of 76.0% (24th), and the status of non-citizens only a value of 26.2% (109th), despite the two statuses necessarily having an equal Internal Value.

Such a discrepancy between those possessing the two statuses of legal attachment to the Latvian state – i.e. that of Latvian citizenship as well as that of "non-citizen of Latvia" – could not but give rise to questions concerning possible discrimination. In September 2008 the [Latvian] Ombudsman completed an investigation into the differences in rights between

---

49   Ibid., para.17. See also European Court of Human Rights, Andrejeva v Latvia, App No 55707/00 (18 February 2009), para 88

50   If one of the parents is a non-citizen and the other one is a foreign national, the parents are entitled to choose non-citizen status for the child, instead of foreign nationality (an administrative practice which imposed only foreign nationality for such cases was recognized as illegal by the Senate of the Supreme Court on 13 April 2005 in Case No SKA-136)

51   Likums par valsts pensijām, pārejas noteikumi [Transitional Provisions of the Law on State Pensions], para.1, LATVIJAS VĒSTNESIS, 182.(465.)nr. (1995)

citizens and "non-citizens". The Ombudsman found that some restrictions on non-citizens were not proportional, such as the ban on "non-citizens" from working as advocates or permit attorneys, from receiving the highest level of clearance for security work, or from being heads or members of the board in the investigative agencies. He also found a disproportionate restriction to the legal limitations on obtaining land property in the cities by "noncitizens". The Ombudsman recommended verifying whether restrictions concerning those rights guaranteed for EU citizens but denied to non-citizens are justified. Such verification has never taken place in practice, however, since the new Ombudsman elected in March 2011 declared that the principle of equality required a differential treatment towards persons in legally different situations, finding that the difference in rights between citizens and "non-citizens" was not of a discriminatory nature, since a legal status of "non-citizens" is not comparable with that of citizens.

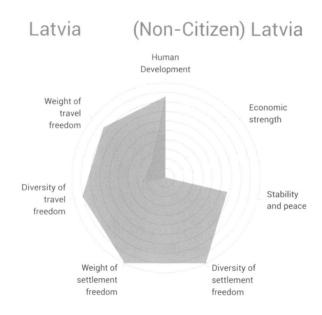

Citizenship-by-Investment

Christian H. Kälin
Henley & Partners

The acquisition of citizenship-by-investment is an accelerating global trend. Rather than through lengthy stays of residence, language tests and other requirements that are typically part of naturalization procedures, countries increasingly offer foreign individuals the option to become citizens if they make a significant direct investment in the country. A few countries have permitted citizenship-by-investment for many years, including Austria and St. Kitts and Nevis, and in recent years more and more countries have started to introduce such options. The following looks at how such countries are positioned in the QNI.

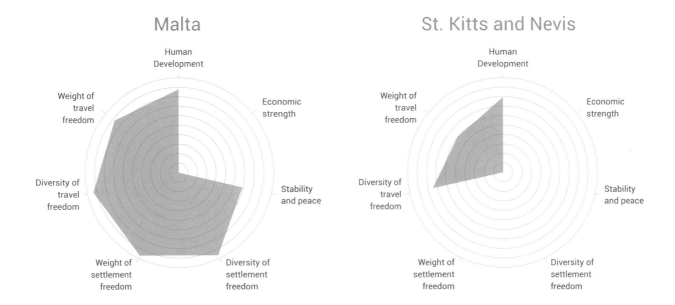

As expected, the European countries – Austria, Cyprus and Malta – come out very high, both in the overall ranking as well as in the very relevant Settlement Freedom Ranking. In every year, Austria is in the top 10 countries, while all three are in the top 10 in the Settlement Freedom ranking. This is no surprise as EU citizenship is exceptionally strong: it gives the right of free movement and settlement in

one of the world's wealthiest regions and largest economic areas with over 500 million people. Accordingly, these three countries also ask the highest price: in Austria, no specific amount is set in law or by regulation, but current practice requires several million Euros in the form of a donation for public purposes or investments that create employment. Malta requires a donation to its National Development and Social Fund of at least EUR 650,000, plus investments in government bonds of EUR 150,000 and real estate of EUR 350,000 or the rental of an equivalent property for at least five years. The least expensive option in Europe is currently Cyprus, which requires a recoverable real estate investment of EUR 2.5 million.

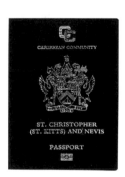

There are now five Caribbean countries which run citizenship-by-investment programs: Antigua and Barbuda, Dominica, Grenada, St. Lucia and St. Kitts and Nevis. They are all part of the Caribbean Community (CARICOM), which provides conditional freedom of movement.[52] This is why the individual CARICOM countries relevant here are ranked much lower in the Settlement Freedom category. This at first seems quite odd as countries like Benin (part of ECOWAS) or the former Soviet republics all rank much higher. However, one should note here that the skills certificate required to avail yourself of the free movement within CARICOM is easily obtainable in practice, *de facto* significantly boosting the quality of nationality of the Caribbean options.

52   As a CARICOM citizen, you also need a skills certificate together with your passport to avail yourself of the freedom of movement. Nationality alone does not qualify

On the QNI General Ranking, the Caribbean countries are well positioned: Antigua and Barbuda ranked high at 58th, just above St. Kitts and Nevis, also ranked high at 59th position, and both well above St. Lucia (86th), Grenada (91st) and Dominica (all ranked in the medium band at 86th, 91st and 93rd respectively). Panama, which does not have a citizenship-by-investment program but a residence program that comes with a non-citizens passport, ranks high and comes in just above Antigua and Barbuda in 57th place. A Caribbean passport can be acquired through contributions to national development funds or the treasury (ranging from USD 100,000 to USD 250,000 for a single applicant, more if dependents are included) or through real estate acquisition (starting at USD 300,000) and is thus one of the best options in the world in terms of "value for money".

Other countries with citizenship-by-investment provisions in their law, such as the Comoros (ranked low at 144th), Montenegro (medium at 65th) and Seychelles (high at 56th), are spread across the QNI. In the Comoros you can acquire economic citizenship (with some limitations to the ordinary citizenship) for as little as USD 45,000, making this currently the cheapest nationality in the world that you can officially acquire through investment. Montenegro and Seychelles both have provisions in the law but are very restrictive in its application, although Montenegro has indicated that it wishes to expand its program. As a country on the path to NATO and EU membership, and already quite well positioned in the 2015 QNI, Montenegro has the highest potential of improvement of all citizenship-by-investment countries: once Montenegro joins the EU, it will catapult its position to the top tier alongside other EU countries.

ANNEX

1   Introduction

The Henley & Partners — Kochenov Quality of Nationality Index (QNI) strives to quantify the quality of nationalities using an objective and, as much as possible, uniform methodology. Accordingly, the Methodology is applied consistently to the overwhelming majority of data. Nationalities for which (sufficiently accurate) data on one or more of the elements was lacking have been excluded from the QNI. However, in limited circumstances, we were able to supplement missing elements of data with reasonable estimations based on other, reliable sources and/or regional averages.

In this section, the methodology of calculating the normalized values of the seven elements is described by the exact formulas that have been applied. A verbal description of these formulas, including examples of the value of specific nationalities, can be found in the Methodology.[53] Moreover, this section describes the deviations from the general methodology that were used to calculate reasonable estimations of specific elements of specific nationalities. The sources and where applicable the justification of the choice for the specific alternatives are mentioned.

In the following paragraphs, the methodology for all seven elements of the QNI is described. Further, deviations from the calculation of Natural Resources Rents, which are excluded from GDP for the purpose of quantifying Economic Strength,[54] are described in a separate paragraph as well. Each of the paragraphs starts with the general formula that has been used to calculate the respective element. Subsequently, a list of deviations per nationality or country (in the case of GDP and NRR calculations) is provided.

---

53   See pp 9

54   See Methodology pp 22

2   Human Development

The normalized Human Development values are calculated using the following formula:

Normalized Human Development value of nationality [X] = (HDI score of country granting nationality [X]) / (HDI score of highest scoring country the nationality of which is also included in the QNI) x 15

Deviations

- Taiwan: HDI calculated by government using the same methodology
    - *http://eng.stat.gov.tw/ct.asp?xItem=25280&ctNode=6032&mp=5*
    2010: 0.873
    2011: 0.874
    2012: 0.879
    2013: 0.882
    2014: value of 2013
    2015: value of 2013

- Macao: HDI calculated by government using the same methodology
    - *http://www.dsec.gov.mo/getAttachment/0d4efddf-7ad1-400c-ae84-7137d9c9df9f/E_MN_PUB_2015_Y.aspx*
    2010: value of 2011
    2011: 0.891
    2012: 0.892
    2013: 0.892
    2014: value of 2013

- San Marino: HDI of Italy has been applied, as it can be reasonably estimated that basic human development is comparable
    For all years: value of Italy

- Monaco: HDI of the highest-scoring country in Europe has been applied, as it can be reasonably estimated that Monaco's basic human development is not surpassed by any other country
    For all years: value of Norway

- Kosovo: HDI is calculated by the United Nations
    - *http://www.undp.org/content/kosovo/en/home/countryinfo.html*
    2010: 0.700
    - *http://www.ks.undp.org/content/dam/kosovo/docs/KHDR/KHDR2012_eng.pdf*
    2011–2012: 0.714
    - *http://hdr.undp.org/sites/default/files/khdr2014english.pdf*
    2013–2014: 0.786

3   Economic Strength

The normalized Economic Strength values are calculated using the following formula:

Normalized Economic Strength value of nationality [X] = (GDP(PPP) − NRR of nationality [X]) / (GDP(PPP) − NRR of nationality of the country with highest (GDP(PPP) − NRR)) * 15

with

GDP(PPP) − NRR of nationality [X] = GDP(PPP) of country granting nationality [X] - ((NRR of country granting nationality [X] * GDP(PPP) of country granting nationality [X]) / 100)

Deviations

Andorra

- 2010 − 2013: based on WB data (non PPP)
- 2014 − 2015: based on WB data from 2013 (non PPP)

Cuba

- 2010 − 2013: based on WB data (non PPP)
- 2014: value of 2013
- 2015: Q4 estimation = 79.62 billion (non PPP)
  - Source: *http://www.tradingeconomics.com/cuba/gdp/forecast*

Liechtenstein

- 2010−2012: based on WB data (non PPP)
- 2013−2014: value of 2012

Macao

- 2010−2014: based on WB data (non PPP)

Monaco

- 2010−2011: based on WB data (non PPP)
- 2012−2014: value of 2011

Palestinian Territory

- For all years based on WB data (West Bank and Gaza) (non PPP)

4   Natural Resources Rents

Deviations

Taiwan

- 0 for all years (estimation)
  - Source: there is no data available on NRR, but: Natural resources are limited to 'small deposits of coal, natural gas, limestone, marble, asbestos, arable land', *https://www.cia.gov/library/publications/the-world-factbook/fields/2111.html* Exploitation seems negligible, see e.g. *http://www.indexmundi.com/energy.aspx?country=tw*

Myanmar

- 2010–2011: value of 2012
- 2014: value of 2013

For some countries, current data was not available. In this case the latest data available is considered. The countries and corresponding dates are:

- Andorra (latest data 2008)
- Cuba (latest data 2011)
- Cyprus (latest data 2012)
- Liechtenstein (latest data 2009)
- Madagascar (latest data 2011)
- Namibia (latest data 2010)
- Syria (latest data 2007)

5 Peace and Stability

Normalized Peace and Stability value of nationality [X] = (GPI score of highest scoring country on GPI the nationality of which is also included in the QNI) / (GPI score of country granting nationality [X]) x 10

Deviations

Andorra
- Average of France and Spain

Antigua and Barbuda
- Average of region: Cuba, Jamaica, Haiti, Dominican Republic and Trinidad and Tobago

Bahamas
- Average of region: Cuba, Jamaica, Haiti, Dominican Republic and Trinidad and Tobago

Barbados
- Average of region: Cuba, Jamaica, Haiti, Dominican Republic and Trinidad and Tobago

Belize
- Value of Mexico

Brunei Darussalam
- Value of Malaysia

Cape Verde
- Average of Senegal, The Gambia and Guinea-Bissau

Comoros
- Average of Tanzania, Mozambique and Madagascar

Dominica
- Average of region: Cuba, Jamaica, Haiti, Dominican Republic and Trinidad and Tobago

Grenada
- Average of region: Cuba, Jamaica, Haiti, Dominican Republic and Trinidad and Tobago

Hong Kong, China (SAR)
- Value of China

Liechtenstein
- Average of Switzerland and Austria

Luxembourg
- Average of Belgium, France and Germany

Macao
- Value of China

Maldives
- Value of Sri Lanka

Malta
- Value of Italy

Monaco
- Value of France

St. Kitts and Nevis
- Average of region: Cuba, Jamaica, Haiti, Dominican Republic and Trinidad and Tobago

St. Lucia
- Average of region: Cuba, Jamaica, Haiti, Dominican Republic and Trinidad and Tobago

St. Vincent and the Grenadines
- Average of region: Cuba, Jamaica, Haiti, Dominican Republic and Trinidad and Tobago

San Marino
- Value of Italy

Sao Tome and Principe
- Average of Gabon and Equatorial Guinea

Seychelles
- Average of Madagascar and Sri Lanka

Suriname
- Value of Guyana

6   Diversity of Travel Freedom

The normalized Diversity of Travel Freedom values are calculated using the following formulas.

- Diversity of travel freedom of nationality [X] = Number of countries that holders of nationality [X] can visit visa-free or by visa on arrival for tourist or business purposes

- Normalized diversity of travel freedom of nationality [X] = (Diversity of travel freedom of nationality [X]) / (Diversity of travel freedom of highest-scoring nationality) * 15

No deviations from this methodology were applied.

7   Weight of Travel Freedom

Weight of Travel Freedom represents the aggregate weighted score of all countries that can be visited visa-free or by visa on arrival for tourist or business purposes. The weighted score of each country is calculated by the sum of its normalized Economic Strength and its Human Development, whereby each of those counts for 50%:

- Weighted score of country [X] = Normalized(GDP(PPP) of country [X] − NRR of country [X]) + Normalized(HDI of country [X])

The Weight of Travel Freedom value of nationality [X] is then calculated as follows:

- Weight of travel freedom of nationality [X] = Sum of the Weighted scores of all countries that holders of nationality [X] can visit visa free or by visa on arrival for tourist or business purposes
- Normalized Weight of travel freedom of nationality [X] = (Weight of travel freedom of nationality [X]) / (Weight of travel freedom of highest-scoring nationality) * 15

Deviations

Countries, territories and dependencies given a minimal weighted score of 0.1 for the purpose of calculating Weight of Travel Freedom and Weight of Settlement Freedom:

1	American Samoa	20	Mayotte
2	Anguilla	21	Monaco
3	Aruba	22	Montserrat
4	Bermuda	23	Nauru
5	Bonaire, St. Eustasius and Saba	24	New Caledonia
6	Cayman Islands	25	Niue
7	Cook Islands	26	Norfolk Islands
8	Taiwan	27	Northern Mariana Islands
9	Curacao	28	Puerto Rico
10	Falkland Islands (Malvinas)	29	Reunion
11	French Guiana	30	San Marino
12	French Polynesia	31	Somalia
13	French West Indies	32	South Sudan
14	Gibraltar	33	St. Maarten
15	Guam	34	Turks and Caicos Islands
16	Korea (Democratic People's Republic)	35	Tuvalu
17	Kosovo	36	Virgin Islands (British)
18	Macao (SAR China)	37	Virgin Islands (US)
19	Marshall Islands		

8 Diversity of Settlement Freedom

The normalized Diversity of Settlement Freedom values are calculated using the following formulas. No deviations from this methodology were applied.

- Diversity of settlement freedom of nationality [X] = Number of countries to which holders of nationality [X] have full access

- Normalized Diversity of settlement freedom of nationality [X] = (Diversity of settlement freedom of nationality [X]) / (Diversity of settlement freedom of highest-scoring nationality) * 15

No deviations from this methodology were applied.

9   Weight of Settlement Freedom

Weight of Settlement Freedom represents the aggregate weighted score of all countries to which a nationality grants full access. The weighted score of each country is calculated by the sum of its normalized Economic Strength and its Human Development, whereby each of those counts for 50%:

- Weighted score of country [X] = Normalized(GDP(PPP) of country [X] − NRR of country [X]) + Normalized(HDI of country [X])

The Weight of Settlement Freedom value of nationality [X] is then calculated as follows:

- Weight of settlement freedom of nationality [X] = Sum of the weighted scores of all countries to which holders of nationality [X] have full access

The normalized Weight of Settlement Freedom value is calculated using the following formula:

- Normalized Weight of settlement freedom of nationality [X] = (Weight of settlement freedom of nationality [X]) / (Weight of settlement freedom of highest scoring nationality) * 15

No deviations from this methodology were applied.

GLOSSARY OF TERMS

Business access

See Tourist and business access

Camouflage passport

A passport issued in the name of a non-existing country, which, therefore, cannot testify to the possession of any existing nationality. Camouflage passports are mostly used for false identification and/or criminal activities, and are generally issued under the name of a country no longer in existence.

See also Fantasy passport

Cut-off date

The time of measurement for the elements of the QNI of a particular year. For Diversity of Settlement Freedom and Weight of Settlement Freedom, the cut-off date is 31 December of the year preceding that of the respective QNI. For all other elements, the cut-off date is 1 May of the year of the respective QNI.

Diversity of Settlement Freedom

The number of countries to which a nationality grants its adult holders full access. This means that the adult holder of a nationality is allowed to work without permission or by virtually automatic permission, or stay by independent means in another country for at least 360 days without having to obtain a visa or with visa on arrival.

The following aspects are not considered in determining whether someone has full access to another country:

- Entitlement to public pension systems
- Entitlement to health care
- Entitlement to social security benefits
- Allowance for family members to join the person in question
- Specific skill qualifications that are required to perform certain professions, particularly of a qualitative nature, e.g., bar qualifications to practice as lawyer, medical qualifications to practice as a doctor, or construction worker qualifications

Diversity of Travel Freedom

The number of countries to which a nationality gives its holders visa-free or visa on arrival tourist and business access. Tourist and business access to a country is limited to a short period of time, usually between one and three months. Almost all countries now require visas from certain non-nationals who wish to have tourist and business access to their territory.

See also Tourist and business access, Visa, Visa-free tourist and business access and Visa on arrival tourist and business access

Economic Strength

The Economic Strength of a nationality represents the scale of the economy to which the nationality is attached. This is measured by the country's share of world Gross Domestic Product (GDP) at Purchasing Power Parity (PPP), excluding rents from the exploitation of natural resources – or so-called Natural Resources Rents (NRR).

See also Gross Domestic Product, Natural Resources Rents and Purchasing Power Parity

External Value

The value of a nationality in terms of the diversity and quality of opportunities that it allows us to pursue outside our countries of origin. External Value is composed of Diversity of Settlement Freedom, Weight of Settlement Freedom, Diversity of Travel Freedom and Weight of Travel Freedom.

See also Diversity of Settlement Freedom, Weight of Settlement Freedom, Diversity of Travel Freedom, and Weight of Travel Freedom

External Value Ranking

The External Value Ranking of the QNI Index ranks nationalities on the basis of four parameters that measure External Value on a 0%–100% scale. Each parameter accounts for 25%.

See also Diversity of Settlement Freedom, Weight of Settlement Freedom, Diversity of Travel Freedom and Weight of Travel Freedom

Fantasy passport

A passport issued in the name of a non-existing country, which, therefore, cannot testify to the possession of any existing nationality. Fantasy passports are mostly used for making political statements.

See also Camouflage passport

Full access

An adult holder of a nationality is allowed to work without permission or by virtually automatic permission, or stay by independent means in another country for at least 360 days without having to obtain a visa or with visa on arrival. The following aspects are not considered in determining whether someone has full access to another country:

- Entitlement to public pension systems
- Entitlement to health care
- Entitlement to social security benefits
- Allowance for family members to join the person in question
- Specific skill qualifications that are required to perform certain professions, particularly of a qualitative nature, e.g., bar qualifications to practice as lawyer, medical qualifications to practice as a doctor, or construction worker qualifications

See also Diversity of Settlement Freedom and Weight of Settlement Freedom

General Ranking

The General Ranking of the Quality of Nationalities Index ranks nationalities on the basis of seven parameters, which gauge both Internal Value (40%) and External Value (60%). The three parameters for Internal Value are: Human Development (15%), Economic Strength (15%) and Peace and Stability (10%), and the four parameters for External Value are: Diversity of Settlement Freedom (15%), Weight of Settlement Freedom (15%), Diversity of Travel Freedom (15%), and Weight of Travel Freedom (15%).

See also Internal Value, External Value, Human Development, Economic Strength, Peace and Stability, Diversity of Settlement Freedom, Weight of Settlement Freedom, Diversity of Travel Freedom and Weight of Travel Freedom

Global Peace Index

The Global Peace Index published by the Institute for Economics & Peace is an annual ranking that measures the peacefulness, stability and harmony of countries by looking at 23 indicators of peace, divided into three domains: ongoing domestic and international conflict, the level of harmony within a nation and the degree of militarization.

Gross Domestic Product

The sum of gross value added by all resident producers in the economy plus any product taxes and minus any subsidies not included in the value of the products.

Human Development

One of the three elements of the Internal Value of nationality. The level of Human Development of a nationality is derived from the country of origin's score in the United Nations Development Programme Human Development Index, which is today's most authoritative ranking of basic human development.

See also Human Development Index

Human Development Index

The United Nations Development Programme Human Development Index is an annual ranking that measures the degree of basic human development of countries by looking at health (life expectancy at birth), education (number of years of schooling) and standard of living (gross national income per capita).

IATA

See International Air Transport Association

International Air Transport Association

The International Air Transport Association (IATA) is the trade association of the overwhelming majority of airlines. IATA maintains IATA TIMATIC, the world's largest and most reliable database of travel information.

See also IATA Timatic

IATA Timatic

The largest and most reliable database of travel information in the world. IATA Timatic is administered by the International Air Transport Association. It contains a comprehensive overview of visa regimes, which is not publicly available.

See also International Air Transport Association

Internal Value

The value of a nationality in terms of the quality of life within the nationality's country of origin. Internal Value comprises three parameters: Human Development, Economic Strength, and Peace and Stability.

See also Human Development, Economic Strength, and Peace and Stability

Mean

The sum of a collection of numbers divided by the number of numbers in the collection. In the QNI, the mean of a collection of nationalities is the sum of the values of those nationalities divided by the number of nationalities in the collection.

Median

The middle point of a collection of numbers, in which half the numbers are above the median and half are below. In the QNI, the median of a collection of nationalities is the value for which half of the nationalities in the collection have a higher value and half of the nationalities have a lower value.

Nationality

An inheritable legal status of attachment to public authority – usually a state – which entitles the holder to a passport or a passport-like travel document.

Natural Resources Rents

The sum of oil rents, natural gas rents, coal rents (hard and soft), mineral rents, and forest rents. Natural Resources Rents are part of GDP, but are excluded in measuring the Economic Strength of a nationality.

See also Economic Strength

Passport

A travel document issued by public authority – usually a state – which certifies the identity and nationality of its holder.

Purchasing Power Parity

The rates of currency conversion that equalize the purchasing power of different currencies by eliminating the differences in price levels between countries. In measuring the Economic Strength of a nationality, Purchasing Power Parity is applied to convert the country of origin's GDP into international dollars. An international dollar possesses the same purchasing power as a US dollar has in the US.

See also Economic Strength and Gross Domestic Product

Peace and Stability

One of the three elements of the Internal Value of a nationality. The level of Peace and Stability of a nationality is derived from the country of origin's score in the Global Peace Index published by the Institute for Economics & Peace.

Settlement access

See Full access

Settlement Freedom Ranking

The Settlement Freedom Ranking of the Quality of Nationalities Index ranks nationalities on the basis of Diversity of Settlement Freedom (50%), and Weight of Settlement Freedom (50%) on a 0–100% scale.

See also Diversity of Settlement Freedom, and Weight of Settlement Freedom

Timatic

See IATA Timatic

Tourist and business access

A holder of a nationality is allowed to visit another country for a short period of time, usually between one and three months. Almost all countries now require visas from certain non-nationals who wish to have tourist and business access to their territory.

See also Visa, Visa-free tourist and business access and Visa on arrival tourist and business access

Travel Freedom Ranking

The Travel Freedom Ranking of the Quality of Nationalities Index ranks nationalities on the basis of Diversity of Travel Freedom (50%), and Weight of Travel Freedom (50%) on a 0%–100% scale.

See also Diversity of Travel Freedom, and Weight of Travel Freedom

Visa

A document allowing an individual to travel to the destination country as far as the port of entry (airport, seaport or land border crossing) and to ask the immigration officer to allow you to enter the country. In most countries the immigration officer has the final authority to permit you to enter. He or she usually also decides how long you can stay for any particular visit.

See also Visa-free tourist and business access and Visa on arrival tourist and business access

Visa-free tourist and business access

No visa is required to ask the immigration officer at the port of entry of a country to be allowed to enter the country for tourist and business purposes.

Visa on arrival tourist and business access

The visa is required to be granted tourist and business access to a country can be acquired at the port of entry of the country itself.

Weight of Settlement Freedom

The combined value of all countries to which a nationality grants its adult holders full access. This is calculated by the sum of these countries' weighted scores on Human Development and Economic Strength, which are each given 50% weight.

Full access to a country means that the adult holder of a nationality is allowed to work without permission or by virtually automatic permission, or stay by independent means in another country for at least 360 days without having to obtain a visa or with visa on arrival. In this regard, entitlement to public pension systems, health care, social security benefits, allowance to family members to join the person in question, and specific skill qualifications that are required to perform certain professions are not considered in determining whether someone has full access to another country.

Weight of Travel Freedom

The combined value of all countries to which a nationality gives its holders visa-free or visa on arrival tourist and business access. This is calculated by the sum of these countries' weighted scores on Human Development and Economic Strength, which are each given 50% weight.

Tourist and business access to a country is limited to a short period of time, usually between one and three months. Almost all countries now require visas from certain non-nationals who wish to have tourist and business access to their territory.

See also Visa-free tourist and business access and Visa on arrival tourist and business access